Gingerbread Ideas

from
The Gingerbread Lady
❤ Patti Hudson

recipes ❤ patterns ❤ parties
❤ Step by step directions ❤

© Patricia L. Hudson 1998 all rights reserved.

> GINGERBREAD
>
> *It is always so nice,*
> *to smell the spice*
> *That she uses in making,*
> *the gingerbread she's baking.*
> *It's not surprising*
> *that it looks so appetizing.*
> *And the taste....*
> *Yum! It's really great!*
>
> Ellen Brislin (age 11)

Gingerbread Ideas
© Patricia L. Hudson 1980 all rights reserved
1998 Fifth Printing
1980, 1982, 1984, 1987, 1998
ISBN 1-880928-02-7

FULTON PRESS, INC.
3 Falcon Lane, Flyway Business Park
Lititz, Pennsylvania 17543-9295

TABLE OF CONTENTS

	PREFACE	5
	INTRODUCTION	6
I.	GINGERBREAD HOUSEMAKING	7
	Preparations for Making a Gingerbread House	8
	Baking Gingerbread House Parts	9-10
	Basic Decorative Icing Skills	11
	Making Decorating Cones	12-13
	Icing Snowmen	14
	Assembling a Gingerbread House	15
	Decorating a Gingerbread House	16
	Preserving a Gingerbread House	17
	Storing a Gingerbread House	17
	A Gingerbread Barn	18-19
	A Gingerbread Covered Bridge	20-22
II.	COOKIE COTTAGES • PARTIES AND WORKSHOPS	23
	Cookie Cottages • No-Bake Houses	25
	Easy Steps to Make Cookie Cottages	26-29
	Parties and Workshops • An Introduction	30
	Giving a Party or Workshop	31-33
	Party Invitations and Name Tags	34
III.	TEACHERS, PARENTS • ACTIVITIES FOR CHILDREN	35
	The Gingerbread Lady • A Picture to Color	36
	A Guide to Gingerbread Land	37
	Anecdotes by The Gingerbread Lady	38-44
	Fairy Tale • "The Gingerbread Quest"	45-50
	Gingerbread Songs	
	"Gingerbread Land"	51
	"The Icing Song"	52
	"My Heart's In This House"	53
	Gingerbread Land • Pictures to Color	54-64
	COLOR PLATES	A,B,C,D
IV.	GINGERBREAD GIFT IDEAS	65
	Gift Ideas for Children	66-67

Table of Contents

    Gingerbread Christmas Tree Ornaments 68-69
    Small Gingerbread Favors 70
    Gingerbread Tree Centerpiece 71
    Gingerbread Sleigh Centerpiece 72-73
    Crocheted Gingerbread Boy and Family 74-75
    A Gingerbread House Cookie 76

V. RECIPES **77**
    Patti's Gingerbread 78
    Tina Strepko's Gingerbread 79
    Whole Wheat Gingerbread 80
    "Delicious Nutritious Gingerbread" 81
    Gingerbread Boy Cookie Treats 82
    Stained Glass Cookies 83
    "Pepparkaor" (Swedish Gingersnaps) 84
    Quantity Gingerbread Boy Cookies 85
    Decorative Royal Icing with Meringue Powder 86
    Sugarless Cream Cheese Icing 87
    Modeling Candy "Clay" 88
    Mashed Potato Candy 89
    Cinnamon Cut Outs 90

VI. PATTERNS **91**
    Heart House 92-93
    Mini Swiss Gingerbread House 94
    Basic Gingerbread House 95-97
    Large Swiss Gingerbread House 98-101
    Grandma's House 102-105
    Victorian Gingerbread House 106-109
    Large A - Frame Gingerbread House 110-111
    Small A - Frame Gingerbread House 112
    Gingerbread Tree Centerpiece 113
    Covered Bridge 114-117
    Gingerbread Church 118-119
    Gingerbread Sleigh 120-121
    A Gingerbread Boy 122
    A Gingerbread Girl 123
    A Gingerbread Pregnant Lady 124
    A Large Gingerbread Boy 125

MAIL ORDER RESOURCES **126**

PREFACE

For years Patti Hudson has been creating delicacies that have thrilled not only the palate but also the sight. Because of her gingerbread creations, talks, programs and workshops in which she shares her talents with others, Patti has become affectionately known as "The Gingerbread Lady." Gingerbread creations have become Patti's trademark. Looking at one of Patti's gingerbread houses – you find yourself smiling as it brings out the child in you.

Creating a gingerbread house can be an activity that draws families together and provides a sense of accomplishment. The wonder of the finished product will be enjoyed by all.

The recipes and patterns enclosed in this book were prepared with the idea of inspiring more novice gingerbread creators. Through her many workshops and appearances, Patti has learned the questions most frequently asked and has attempted to make this guide readable, workable and understandable.

Gingerbread ideas are many and varied, as you will discover working your way through this book. Patti is sharing here what she has learned. She wants each of you to discover that you too, can have fun making a gingerbread creation. Her motto is, "Gingerbread houses don't have to be perfect."

Gingerbread is for everyone, from the very old to the very young. Plan to make your creations not only for someone you love, but with someone you love.

Bring the joy of gingerbread making to your home as I did after meeting Patti. It's as simple as turning the page.

Sally Bair

LANCASTER FARMING Newspaper

Introduction

Welcome to the MAGICAL LAND OF GINGERBREAD!

Gingerbread Ideas came about because of the enthusiastic contributions and encouragement from the many friends I have made through the years while teaching and sharing my joy of gingerbread housemaking. The following pages include "how-to" gingerbread ideas including traditional gingerbread houses, a barn, a covered bridge, a sleigh and cookie cottages made with graham crackers. There are gingerbread songs, stories and pictures to color for children. I hope you enjoy trying some of these offerings. Do go on to expand upon these ideas, adding your own unique ideas. You can make for yourself, your family and friends a fun-filled gingerbread land.

Through years of teaching, I have come to realize that there is not just "one way" to do anything. I offer *Gingerbread Ideas* to get you started and then I encourage you to find "your way" to do things, just as I encourage my students in classes and work-shops. I believe *teachers* must be facilitators, creating an atmosphere to enable students to touch into what they *know* and bring forth their own creativity. I hope this book inspires you to do some adventuring and creating. I believe the *magic* is not in the finished product, it is in *you, your doing, your creating.* For me the *fun* is in sharing with others what I enjoy and love doing.

In the fairy tale, *THE GINGERBREAD QUEST,* by Sheila Audet, you will meet my two puppet friends, Yellow and Green (created and illustrated by Samantha West). I met Yellow and Green when I was making the video, **The Joy of Gingerbread Housemaking**. They delighted me and my viewers. Children who see the video, *Gingerbread Land* become instant fans of these charming puppets.

I cannot ever thank the following people enough for their contributions to this book. Without my husband, Suter's computer expertise and the unbelievable number of hours he worked with me, the last two editions of this book would never have been printed. Alisa Bair's songs and music enhance this book and have enriched hundreds of gingerbread parties, programs and my first two videos, touching the hearts of children and adults. Illustrations and gingerbread pictures for children to color were contributed by Elizabeth House McClung, Ceci Good and Sharron Eckel. My sincere appreciation also goes to Darryl Nicholas (photographer), Susan Doyle, Tina Strepko, Sally Bair, Jeff Dow, Mary Lane, Janet Rackozy Hudson, Sheila Audet, Jo-an Glasse, Samantha West, Mildred Suter Hudson, Shirley and Marc Lemon, Ellen and John Brislin, Dixie, Austin and Alex Heacock and Dottie Papez.

I lovingly dedicate this book to all the children, including my daughter Linda and my son John, who have helped me to have fun, and be adventuresome making gingerbread houses. They enabled me to become a Gingerbread Lady. My granddaughter, Esther Rae will soon be teaching me some new gingerbread ideas.

Patti Fisher Hudson

I. Gingerbread Housemaking

I. Gingerbread Housemaking

PREPARATIONS

FOR MAKING A GINGERBREAD HOUSE

Making a gingerbread house is fun for adults, teenagers and children. It is a great activity for families or a group of friends, and usually becomes a family holiday tradition. Like any craft, gingerbread housemaking is time consuming. Allow several days to accomplish all of the steps.

First, carefully read the directions to become familiar with procedures and materials involved in constructing a gingerbread house. Novices may wish to consider making cookie cottages (pages 25-29). Constructing these small houses from graham crackers is an excellent way to develop skills and learn techniques required in making a large gingerbread house.

Next, choose the house pattern that best suits your needs. (Patterns: pages 90-112). The Heart House pattern (pages 92-93) is a good beginner's house. Draw your house pattern on lightweight cardboard or heavy brown paper. You may also copy the patterns using a commercial copy machine. The copied pattern pages can be covered on both sides with clear Con-Tact© paper before cutting out the patterns.

Now, select the base on which you will build your gingerbread house. A large bread or pastry board, metal tray or heavy cookie sheet can be used. A base can be made of heavy cardboard that does not bend - (two layers may be needed). Cover with aluminum foil for an attractive, festive appearance. Dimensions of bases are suggested on house patterns.

Finally, select the gingerbread recipe. The Gingerbread Lady's first choice is the basic, "PATTI'S GINGERBREAD" recipe (page 78). Carefully read the gingerbread and icing recipes to see the required ingredients. Make a grocery list for the items you will need.

I. Gingerbread Housemaking

BAKING GINGERBREAD HOUSE PARTS

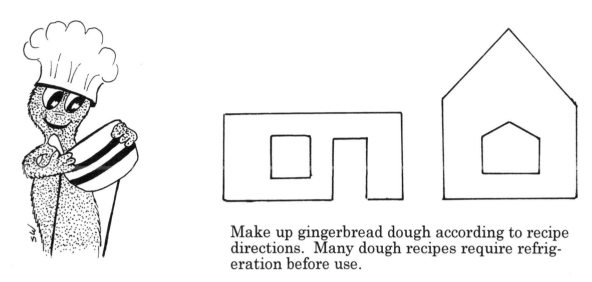

Make up gingerbread dough according to recipe directions. Many dough recipes require refrigeration before use.

Preheat oven to 350°.

Very lightly coat cookie sheets with spray-on shortening. Spread shortening uniformly with a paper towel. If you use pans with sides they should be used upside down.

Lightly flour the rolling pin but not cookie sheets.

Place a damp kitchen towel or dishcloth under the cookie sheet to hold it in place while rolling out dough. Roll out one portion of the dough DIRECTLY ON THE COOKIE SHEET, making it 3/8-inch thick.

Place house-front pattern piece on the dough. Cut around pattern edges, door and windows with a paring knife. Remove excess dough from around edges of pattern, but DO NOT remove dough from door and windows. Repeat this procedure for the back and two sides of the house.

Press together pieces of excess dough from trimmings into two rectangular blocks. These will be used to make the roof. Refrigerate until ready to bake.

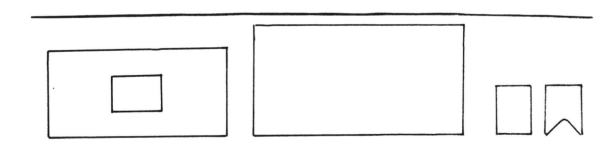

BAKING GINGERBREAD HOUSE PARTS (Continued)

Start baking when house parts have been cut out. Bake for 12 to 15 minutes. Touch test in the center of the house part for doneness. If an impression remains, bake for an additional 2 to 3 minutes.

Immediately after removing the baked gingerbread house-part from the oven, cut around the outlines of windows and door with a knife. Carefully lift out the door and window pieces with the knife. While hot the window pieces can be cut into thirds for shutters or stepping stones. Allow the large house parts to cool briefly on the baking sheet.

Roll out the dough for two roof pieces and use the remaining trimmings for four chimney pieces. As chimney parts will require only 6 to 8 minutes to bake, they should be baked on a separate cookie sheet - NOT ON THE SAME COOKIE SHEET WITH HOUSE PARTS.

The remaining dough is wonderful for making gingerbread boys and girls, trees, animals and other shapes. These figures can be used inside or around the house.

If the house is not to be assembled immediately parts should be placed in an airtight container. A tin, or box sealed in a plastic bag can be used. Insert dividers (foil covered cardboard) between layers of house parts since they are fragile.

I. Gingerbread Housemaking

BASIC DECORATIVE ICING SKILLS

There are many techniques for applying icing when constructing and decorating gingerbread houses. Delightful results are possible using knives, spatulas and toothpicks. Although cake decorating experience is not necessary, it is helpful. Plastic or metal cake decorators can be used. "Throw-away cones" of parchment paper or freezer paper are recommended. (Waxed paper cones are not strong enough and will often tear or break open). Parchment paper triangles to make icing decorator cones are available (two sizes: 12-inch and 15-inch) from stores or mail order catalogs. Refer to Mail Order Resources (page 126). Instructions for making paper cones are found on page 12.

To make decorating cones from freezer paper, cut paper into 12 or 15 inch squares. Cutting each square across the diagonal makes two triangles. The 12-inch triangle makes a small cone; this size fits children's hands. Two large (15-inch) cones, filled with white icing, are required to construct a basic gingerbread house (pages 95-97).

One batch of Royal icing (white) is required to construct a small or medium size gingerbread house. Divide a second batch into small portions in small dishes and tint with food colors as desired. Keep dishes covered with damp cloths or plastic wrap to prevent icing from drying out. Use liquid food colors for creating pastel icing shades. For dark colored icing use paste food colors (available from stores and mail order, page 126).

Only a few decorating tips are required for basic gingerbread housemaking. Five plastic couplers increase the versatility of a decorating tip set. Below basic tips and their uses are listed.

BEGINNER'S BASIC DECORATING TIPS or TUBES

Tip No.	Name	Suggested Uses
1, 2	Plain	Small gingerbread people and fine details
3	Plain	Draw windows, trim shutters.
4	Plain	Large shutters, curtains, lattice work on roofs, window box outlines, snowmen hats, dot trims.
7	Plain	Snowmen and large decorations.
16	Star	Roof shingles (scallop trim around M&Ms and chocolate nonpareils) bushes, ice cream cone trees, trim on gingerbread trees, flower boxes and wreaths.
67, 68	Leaf	Curtains, ice cream cone trees.

Plain Tip   Star Tip   Leaf Tip

I. Gingerbread Housemaking

MAKING DECORATING CONES

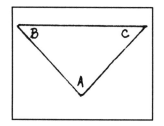

Place one parchment or freezer paper triangle on flat surface with point facing you.

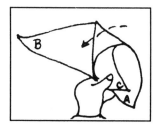

Place index finger of left hand on paper between B and C. Pick up paper at point C with right hand and curl (point C) under bringing it toward you until points A and C meet, creating a cone-shape.

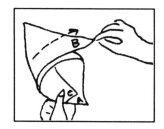

Hold points C and A together with your left hand. Pick up point B with your right hand. Wrap B around to meet points A and C in the back forming a tight cone.

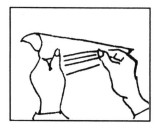

Fold down twice or staple loose ends (A, B and C). Tape outside seam of cone with transparent tape or masking tape to help hold it together.

Fill cone one-half full with icing (1). Close cone as illustrated pressing paper tightly together (2). Secure tightly with 5-inch twister tie (3). Experienced decorators may prefer to fold cone down to close.

 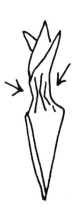 

      1   2   3

I. Gingerbread Housemaking

DECORATING CONES (Continued)

After the decorating cone is filled with icing, snip off the pointed end of the cone with scissors to form an 1/8 inch opening. This produces a cone suitable for outlining and fine decorating (drawing windows on cookie cottages, etc.). A slightly larger opening is required for constructing gingerbread houses. A piece of transparent tape placed on the seam near the cut opening assures even icing flow while creating designs.

If no metal or plastic decorator tips are available, a series of tiny V's can be cut at the tip opening of the decorator cone. This will cause the icing to create a design as it is squeezed from the cone (for trimming house roofs or decorating gingerbread trees or gumdrop bushes.

Using commercial metal or plastic decorating tips (page 11): cut off ½ inch of the tip of a decorating cone so that approximately ½ of the length of the tip will protrude when the tip is dropped into the paper cone. The tip is secured in place with a small amount of icing placed into the cone with a table knife or narrow spatula. Continue filling the cone to about ½ full and close as previously directed (page 12).

Plastic couplers (couplings) are recommended for use in paper cones with decorator tips. They secure the tip in place and allow for the changing of the tip sizes or designs (eliminating the necessity of a cone for every tip). To help determine the amount to cut from the end of the paper cone to use a coupler, first insert the large half of the coupler into the wrapped, uncut cone, then mark with a pencil on the cone the location of the coupler threads. Remove the coupler piece and cut the opening in the paper cone at the marks. Reinsert the large half of the coupler in the cone, place the decorating tip on the coupler and install the collar. Fill the cone ½ full with icing and close as previously described.

It is very important to hold the filled cone near the top (at the twister tie), squeezing from the top. For most decorating, hold the cone at a 45° angle. Some decorations require holding the cone straight up and down. Practice making some icing decorations on waxed paper before making them on your gingerbread house.

Illustrations and part of directions for making and filling a decorator cone were adapted from "Cake Decorating" a 4-H Project, Pennsylvania State Cooperative Extension Service, Lancaster, Pennsylvania.

I. Gingerbread Housemaking

ICING SNOWMEN

Icing Snowman Drawings by Tony Roda

Icing snowmen are created with a stiff white icing using a parchment cone. If decorator tips are available, use a #7 tip for the body, and a #4 tip for the hat. The best results are achieved if snowmen are made in advance on waxed paper squares and if each stage of the snowman is allowed to dry. The hat is made with colored icing. The snowman's eyes, mouth and buttons are made with icing or, after the snowman has dried, they can be made by using a toothpick dipped in food coloring. Children like to make hats using small candies. When snowmen must be used before they have time to dry, make them on small flat candies (Necco wafers, Andes mints) or on small pieces of graham crackers.

See icing snowmen beside Victorian Gingerbread House – Color Plate A.

I. Gingerbread Housemaking

ASSEMBLING A GINGERBREAD HOUSE

Assembling and decorating a gingerbread house is exciting and fun.

Mix decorative icing (Recipe: page 86) which will serve as the "mortar" to hold the house together. Cover icing with a damp cloth or plastic wrap while not being used

Assemble the house parts on the base. Join the house walls by using a generous amount of icing on the bottom and side edges of each piece. Apply the icing with a knife, with metal or plastic cake decorators or parchment paper cones (pages 12 - 13). After the first two house sides are standing, put extra icing inside the house at the corners. If working alone, use a jar or can to support the sides while the icing hardens. Place candy sticks or small candy canes into the icing at the four corners inside and outside of the house; these add decoration and help support the house. Be sure icing is sticky when placing candies. Allow about an hour for the house-side icing to become firm before adding the roof. This is a good time to decorate the gingerbread people and make three-dimensional trees (page 70). One tree can be decorated like a Christmas tree.

Decorating the inside of the house is optional. This must be done before the roof is put on the house. Suggestions: a decorated gingerbread Christmas tree, icing window curtains, gingerbread or candy furniture, gingerbread cookie people (they can be "glued" with icing inside each open window and can be seen looking out the window from outside the house).

For the "Roof Raising", generously apply icing to the top edges of house side pieces; attach one side of the roof. Add additional icing along roof peak and add the second roof piece. While the icing sets, it may be necessary to hold the roof in place or support it with boxes or tins to keep it from slipping. It is important to check under roof eaves, adding additional icing to any open spaces between roof and house. Candies added to the icing under the roof eaves help seal the space where the roof and house are attached; they also look decorative.

Construct the chimney. First, apply icing to the chimney piece which has the triangle cut-out and attach to the roof peak. Next, apply icing generously along two edges of one of the rectangular chimney pieces. Attach it to an iced edge of the triangular cutout piece already in place. Repeat, adding the other two chimney pieces and use a generous amount of icing on all edges and inside the chimney corners. Candies can be placed in the icing at the chimney corners. (Cinnamon Hots and Dynamints work well here). Icing lines drawn on the chimney sides look like bricks.

Apply icing along one edge of the door piece and attach to the house.

I. Gingerbread Housemaking

DECORATING THE GINGERBREAD HOUSE

Use your imagination as you decorate your house. It may be helpful to try out your decorating ideas before hand using the gingerbread house picture (page 61) and the color, cut and paste decorations (page 60).

Mix a new batch of icing; add and beat in any left-over icing from assembling the house. Beat to soft peaks.

Decorate the sides of the house first. Make designs with icing or attach candies with "generous dabs" of icing. Attach shutters with icing; trim windows with icing snow, candies or make window boxes with icing or candies. Add an icing door knob and icing wreath to the door.

Roofs offer unlimited decorating possibilities. Here are some examples. Spread entire roof with white icing for snow (along roof edges pull icing down in peaks to form icicles). Sprinkle icing with chocolate jimmies or colorful cookie sprinkle trims. Arrange candies on the icing to look like shingles. Create designs with cookies, candies and icing. Suggestions for candies are: M&Ms, gumdrops, nonpareil chocolate wafers, Necco wafers, jelly beans. Some hard candies will melt when coming in contact with the moisture in the icing. Prevent this by allowing the icing on the roof to harden, then adding the candy with a small amount of icing. Instead of candies, consider decorating the house roof with nuts, raisins, cereals, cookies, and a variety of pretzels. A combination of these, with candies, can produce interesting appealing results.

The last area to be decorated should be the gingerbread house yard. Spread the exposed base around the house with icing ...like frosting a cake. White icing for snow is used for a winter scene, green icing for grass. For a walkway, sprinkle with chocolate jimmies. Make stepping stone paths of candies, gingerbread pieces or pretzels. Three dimensional gingerbread trees pre-constructed as explained on page 68; ice cream cones or lightweight cardboard cones, iced green and decorated with snow or candies as trees; trees made with spearmint leaves or gum drops put together with icing are all possible decorations for gingerbread house yards. Add decorated gingerbread boys and girls (or decorate after placing in yard). Stand them by attaching a gumdrop or spearmint leaf to the back of the cookie with icing. Stacks of logs can be made with Tootsie Rolls or pretzels. Gingerbread animals, sleighs, icing snowmen (pages 14 and 104), spearmint leaf bushes, and pretzel or candy fences complete this edible creation.

I. Gingerbread Housemaking

PRESERVING A GINGERBREAD HOUSE

Gingerbread houses can be successfully preserved by spraying them with an acrylic decoupage spray. It is very important that the house be thoroughly dry before spraying. A freshly made house should be allowed "to set" for ten hours or more at room temperature in a dry environment. In some climates air-conditioning and/or dehumidification must be used to insure that the house is sufficiently dry for satisfactory preservation.

CAUTION: Some chocolate candies are adversely affected by the decoupage spray. (Chocolate with nonpareils and M&Ms are OK.) Test other chocolate candies before spraying the house.

STORING A GINGERBREAD HOUSE

Humidity and heat are enemies of gingerbread houses. The ideal way to store a gingerbread house is by placing it in a Plexiglas or glass case. This storage method allows the house to be displayed while in storage. This case must be kept in a relatively cool, dry place.

The most economical method of storage is to place the gingerbread house in a sturdy cardboard box with a lid. Use a box as close to the size of the house as possible. Put box in double, heavy duty plastic bags and close securely with a twister tie. Store in a COOL, DRY, "SAFE" place. Even when gingerbread houses are packaged this way they still may not be mice, dog or cat proof!

THE GINGERBREAD LADY'S PHILOSOPHY:

"Gingerbread Houses are made to be eaten!"

"After the holidays or special occasion, and everyone has enjoyed looking at your creation, allow your family and friends the fun of nibbling and eating your gingerbread house. Schools and nursing homes welcome gingerbread houses as gifts to be eaten – even after the holidays."

I. Gingerbread Housemaking

A GINGERBREAD BARN

Mix one batch of PATTI'S GINGERBREAD (Recipe: page 78). See directions for baking a gingerbread house (pages 9-10). Use the basic gingerbread house pattern (pages 95-97). Bake the four house sides and two roof pieces. Do not cut out original house door and windows on the pattern. Instead, score-cut large barn size doors and windows with a knife before baking (pictured on page 19). Do not cut out after baking. With left over dough bake gingerbread animal cookies using barnyard animal patterns (page 19) or commercial cookie cutters.

Assemble barn with icing following directions for Assembling a "Gingerbread House" (page 15). Draw on the gingerbread, with icing, the large barn doors and windows. Allow barn icing to dry one hour or longer before spreading white icing snow on the roof. At one end of the barn you may wish to create a "barnyard" with a fence constructed of pretzels or gingerbread pieces. Decorated gingerbread animal cookies (cows, horses, pigs, etc.) can be placed in the iced barnyard. Chocolate jimmies can be sprinkled in the barnyard and in front of the barn doors. Spearmint leaf trees, candy bushes, a gingerbread boy farmer, a gingerbread dog and/or cat can be placed around the barn. To create a Pennsylvania Dutch barn, a hex sign of candies or colored icing can be made on the barn side, under the roof peak. Add icing icicles along the edges of the roof.

I. Gingerbread Housemaking

GINGERBREAD BARN (Continued)

19

I. Gingerbread Housemaking

A GINGERBREAD COVERED BRIDGE

Before making a gingerbread covered bridge, carefully read through Preparation For Making A Gingerbread House (page 8). Since this is a more advanced project than most gingerbread houses, it is recommended that at least one or two gingerbread houses be made before constructing a covered bridge.

Mix two batches of PATTI'S GINGERBREAD recipe (page 78), or Tina Strepko's Gingerbread Recipe (page 79); refrigerate as directed.

Make up the covered bridge patterns (pages 114-117) on lightweight cardboard. Make a base (20 inches by 18 inches) of several thicknesses of heavy cardboard covered with aluminum foil or use a wooden base covered with foil. A 20 inch square base allows more space for extensive "landscaping".

Read over directions for baking gingerbread house parts (page 9 and 10). Bake covered bridge parts, rolling the dough out ¼ inch thick (this will make a stronger bridge). Cut around pattern doors and windows in dough (leaving them in place for baking). Use a long, straight knife to cut lines, simulating boards, as shown on the pattern pieces of the four bridge walls.

The pieces will take five to eight minutes longer to bake than gingerbread house pieces. After baking, while still hot, cut around the doors and windows a second time; remove them while still warm. Cool on baking sheet; loosen pieces from baking sheet by running a metal spatula under them as they cool.

SAVE cut out window pieces and cut each door piece into four sections as pattern shows. These pieces will be used for the bridge foundations.

After all bridge parts are baked, use the remainder of dough to bake: one extra window square piece (for making bridge foundations), gingerbread sleighs, horses, people, trees, tiny hearts, animals and ducks. Commercial cookie cutters are available for some designs or patterns can be drawn and made from cardboard (Horse and Sleigh patterns page 117 or 22).

Place the gingerbread bridge base piece (the bridge floor) on waxed paper on a flat tray or baking sheet. Using generous amounts of icing construct the four walls of the bridge on the gingerbread bridge base piece. Brown candy sticks placed into the icing at the four corners will help strengthen the bridge. At this time, using icing, attach the four bridge wall supports inside the bridge walls between the windows. Before putting on the roof a gingerbread sleigh and horse can be placed inside the bridge. Install the roof with generous application of icing. Allow to harden and dry for at least six hours or overnight.

I. Gingerbread Housemaking

COVERED BRIDGE (Continued)

Make five bridge foundations from the fifteen gingerbread squares (window and cut door pieces). Glue three pieces together with Royal icing (like a three tier sandwich cookie), repeat four times. Ice the sides, one at a time, with white icing, putting broken pieces of gray Necco Wafers into the icing to look like stones. To dry, place each completed foundation on waxed paper for several hours or overnight. The stone effect can also be created with gray icing.

Mark with a pencil the outline of a curving, six-inch-wide river on the aluminum foil-covered base. Build two-inch-high river banks and landscape of Styrofoam which will later be covered with foil and icing. These will support the ends of the bridge.

As a trial, to see how the dry bridge looks and fits, place two bridge foundations next to riverbanks and one in the center of the river. Temporarily place bridge on them. Remove the bridge and make any needed adjustments in the styrofoam banks. A second check for fit may be necessary. Remove bridge foundations. Tape or glue the styrofoam pieces to the base and cover with foil pressed into shape. Secure in place with masking tape.

COVERED BRIDGE (Continued)

Spread blue icing between the riverbanks and in the shape of the river design. Spread white icing on the sides of the bank since they will be inaccessible after the bridge is in place.

Put the bridge foundations in place before the blue icing dries; place gingerbread ducks in river if desired. Blue sugar can be sprinkled on the blue icing river before the icing hardens, but AFTER foundations and ducks are in place. Be sure the foundations are level and the same height. If necessary, adjust with icing and flat Necco candies. Generously ice the top of foundations and along the banks where the bridge will attach. Place the bridge permanently in position, adding additional icing where needed to secure bridge.

Decorate the sides, ends and roof of the bridge. The roof can be covered with white icing to resemble snow, adding icing icicles along the roof end and side edges. Another way to decorate the roof is to apply gray or red icing with a decorator tip to look like shingles. The pictured covered bridge (page 21 or 115) has a roof shingled with Quaker Life cereal (Chex cereals can be used). White icing snow has been added with a knife to give the effect of snow drifts on the roof peaks coming down over the shingles.

Cover the remaining exposed foil by spreading generously with white icing snow. Gingerbread trees, spearmint leaves, gumdrops, green M&Ms and other candies can be placed at the ends of the bridge and along the riverbanks. There are many other decorative possibilities: another gingerbread horse and sleigh outside the bridge, gingerbread boys and girls, icing snowmen (page 14) and animals. This creation is indeed a unique, edible, country winter scene.

See A Gingerbread Covered Bridge – Color Plate B.

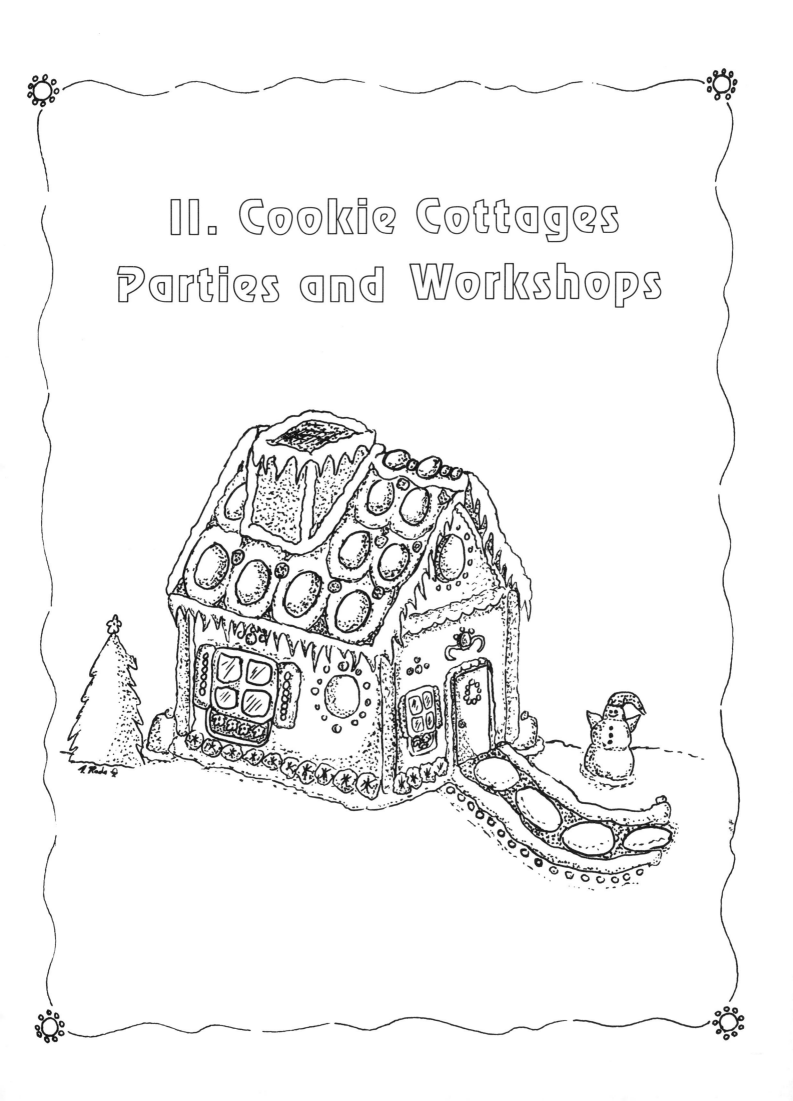

II. Cookie Cottages – Parties and Workshops

Rachel Dow - Shanna Ernst and Patti Hudson - Upper Right, Heather Finkbiner

COOKIE COTTAGES • NO-BAKE HOUSES

Cookie Cottages are mini-gingerbread houses made with graham crackers. Building a miniature house of graham crackers requires exactly the same basic process as building a large gingerbread house. This is a good starting point for the beginner. Learning to handle the icing and getting graham cracker house parts to stick together and stand up "builds up" the confidence and skill of the builder.

Both children and adults enjoy creating these charming small houses. Although manual dexterity does vary with children, seven and eight year olds usually can manage building these houses after watching a "how-to" demonstration. It is helpful to have them work together in teams of two. They can take turns helping to hold one another's house pieces during the different stages of construction. A six-year old needs adult help to build a cottage but can easily decorate it independently. When doing a workshop with children, three to four years old, it is best that the cottages be made ahead of time and allowed to dry. These younger children will take about an hour to decorate their house and the yard.

Cookie cottages are great gifts for children or adults. A homemade gift is undoubtedly a joy for the giver and the receiver. Children can give their very own creations to grandparents, teachers and friends. Shut-ins and nursing home residents find cookie cottages fascinating and intriguing. They are marvelous conversation pieces with nurses and friends!

The next ten pages give detailed instructions for making cookie cottages and for organizing workshops or parties where the cottages are made by groups of children or adults.

II. Cookie Cottages - Parties and Workshops

EASY STEPS TO MAKE COOKIE COTTAGES

1. Make bases for the cottages.

   Cut rigid cardboard into squares or rectangles; 6 inches by 6 inches (small yard), 6 inches by 8 inches (medium yard), 8, 9, or 10 inch squares (large yard). Cover cardboard with aluminum foil; tape the foil to the bottom of the cardboard. (Alternatives to cardboard bases can be Styrofoam trays or heavy paper plates).

2. Cut graham crackers for house parts.

   Plain or cinnamon grahams can be used. Some cinnamon grahams are sugared so heavily that icing won't stick. Nabisco brand grahams are recommended.

   Check all packages of grahams to see if some crackers are broken in half. These broken halves can be used for the sides of the houses.

   Cut grahams on dotted lines as indicated in drawings (page 28). Use a serrated-edged knife; cut with a "sawing motion" for minimal breakage.

   One house requires 4 whole graham crackers. One box of grahams makes 7 to 8 houses (approximately 33 crackers per box)

3. Putting the cottage together.

   Royal icing (recipe: page 86) is recommended; however, butter cream icing or commercial icings can be used successfully for cottages that will be eaten within two days.

   "Glue", with icing, the four sides of the cottage (graham halves) to the base and to each other at the corners. Refer to diagrams (page 28). Apply the icing generously on three edges of one square graham (house side). This can be done in a number of ways: with a knife, by squeezing icing from plastic or parchment cones, or using cake decorators of metal or plastic. Use small glasses or jars to support cottage sides (to keep them from falling) until all four sides are in place. When working in groups, have one person hold the first side while the other puts icing on the second side. Put extra icing inside the four corners of the cottage sides to strengthen it. Candy pieces or sticks placed in the soft icing at the outside corners help support the cottage and are also decorative. Place a few candies or cookies inside the cottage to provide a delightful surprise when the house is eaten.

EASY STEPS (Continued)

Next attach the graham triangles which provide the slanted edges to support the roof. Ripple a zig-zag ledge of icing on the top edges of the front and back of the house (diagram: page 29). Place the long edge of the graham triangles onto these icing ledges. Ripple zig-zag ledges of icing along two triangle edges and one house-side edge. Place one graham roof piece on these iced ledges. Repeat application of icing along the remaining four edges (including long roof ridge) and then put second roof piece in place.

4. Decorating the cottage sides.

   Doors, windows and shutters can be drawn on cottages with icing or made from pieces of cut grahams, Quaker Life or Chex cereals, chocolate Andes mints or other candies.

5. Decorating the roof.

   Many designs can be made on the roof with icing and the addition of candies, cereals, nuts, or raisins. Chimneys can be built from cut graham pieces or by using cereals or candies. (A Hershey kiss makes an easy, one-step chimney).

6. Creating the cottage yard.

   Spread icing on the base around the cottage as you would frost a cake. Use white icing for a winter snow scene; green icing for grass in a spring, summer or fall scene. Walkways can be made with stepping stone candies, Jimmies or Sprinkles. Flower or vegetable gardens are made with icing and candies. Spearmint leaves and gum drops make excellent trees and bushes. Fences, lamp posts, lawn furniture, bird baths and unlimited ideas can be designed and creatively added to the yard. Icing snowmen (page 14) and Gummy bears are delightful additions. Every cottage is an original for no two are ever exactly alike.

II. Cookie Cottages - Parties and Workshops

EASY STEPS (Continued)

Four Whole Graham Crackers Make One Cookie Cottage.

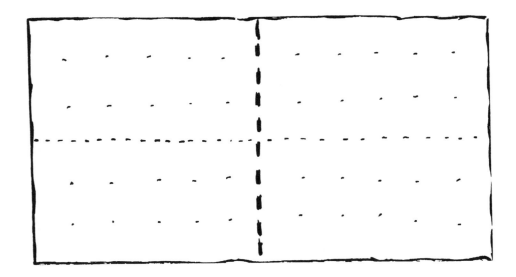

Cut 2 whole graham crackers in half to make 4 house sides.

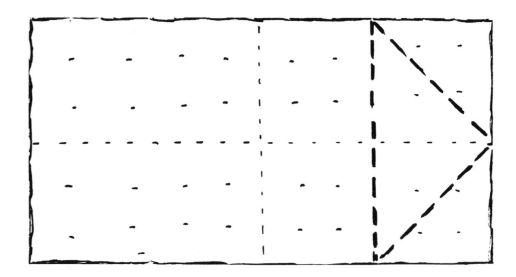

Cut 1/4th from one whole graham cracker. The large rectangle will make 1 roof piece. Repeat, with another whole graham for the second roof piece. Cut the remaining 2 small pieces into triangles as shown in the diagram. These will support the roof.

EASY STEPS (Continued)

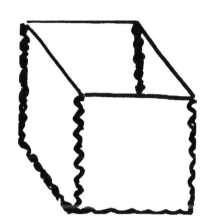

Begin house assembly. Using a generous amount of icing, "glue" the four sides of the house (graham halves), one at a time, to the base and to each side of the grahams at the corners.

Ripple a ziz-zag ledge of icing on the tip edges of both front and back of house pieces. Place the long edge of the triangles onto these icing ledges.

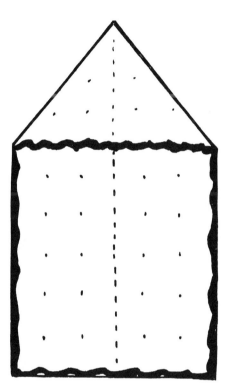

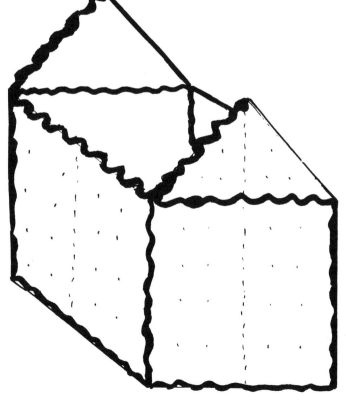

Ripple ziz-zag ledges of icing along two triangle edges and one house side edge. Place one graham roof piece on these iced edges. Repeat application of icing along the remaining four edges (including long roof ridge) and then put second roof piece in place. Add extra icing along the roof ridge.

NOW YOU HAVE A COOKIE COTTAGE READY TO DECORATE!

II. Cookie Cottages - Parties and Workshops

PARTIES AND WORKSHOPS • AN INTRODUCTION

Invite friends to a party or arrange a workshop for church, school, scout or 4-H groups to create their own Cookie Cottages (mini-gingerbread houses made of graham crackers). This also is a wonderful birthday party for children. Six-year-old children to "adult kids" of all ages have a marvelous time constructing their original cottages and are always thrilled with their creations. Party themes can be developed from all seasons of the year. Examples are: Halloween, Christmas, winter holidays, Valentine's Day, Easter and spring holidays.

All of the materials needed to give a workshop or party and suggestions "what to do ahead of time" are given in this book (pages 31 to 33). Keep your first program simple. Later, you can add more complexity with suggestions from this book or from your own ideas that tie in with the holiday or gingerbread theme. Practice making a cookie cottage before the party to refine your cottage-building skills. This will give you an extra house or two for use if problems arise during your workshop.

II. Cookie Cottages - Parties and Workshops

GIVING A PARTY OR WORKSHOP

THINGS TO DO AHEAD:

Make your own original party invitations or use example (page 34). Make name tags or place cards. Gingerbread boys and girls or gingerbread houses can be used (page 34). Large gingerbread boys and girls of brown paper can be made to decorate the room and front door (pages 122, 123 and 125).

Make cardboard bases (6 to 10 inches square) on which to build houses. Cover the cardboard squares with aluminum foil. Use tape to attach foil to underside of cardboard.

Purchase ingredients for making icing. Purchase graham crackers (one box makes 7 to 8 houses). Shop for an assortment of small candies, cereals (Quaker Life, Chex, Cheerios), pretzels, animal crackers, nuts, raisins, cookie decorator trims (chocolate jimmies, colorful sprinkles, colored sugars and brownulated sugar).

Make up cones of parchment paper to hold icing (pages 12 and 13). Two or three cones will be needed for each participant and several extra for demonstration. The number of icing colors to be used will determine the number of parchment cones needed. Small heavy-duty plastic baggies can be substituted for parchment cones.

Cut grahams for cookie cottage parts (page 28). Grahams cut for each complete house can be put into individual baggies ready for each participant. (Store these in an airtight container). Cut three or four extra house parts to have ready in case of breakage.

Place a variety of small candies in two plastic baggies for each participant. Put moist candies (gum drops, gummy bears, spearmint leaves, etc.) in one bag, and dry candies (M&Ms, cinnamon hots, Dynamints, hard candies, etc.) in the other bag to prevent them from sticking together. Store bags of candy in tins. The bags do not have to contain exactly the same number or color of candies. Participants can be encouraged to trade and share candies as needed.

Royal Icing with meringue powder (p. 86) can be made several days ahead – refrigerate. Rebeat before using.

II. Cookie Cottages - Parties and Workshops

PARTY OR WORKSHOP (Continued)

THINGS TO DO AHEAD (Continued):

Collect shoe boxes or small cardboard boxes to hold each participant's finished house. Small cake boxes purchased from a bakery are ideal. Bases should be made to fit the selected boxes.

The *Gingerbread Land* video, or *The Joy of Gingerbread Housemaking* video (The cookie cottage segment) provides an interesting highlight when shown at the beginning of a party or workshop. To order, see page 126.

The Cookie Cottage directions (pages 26-29), icing recipe (page 86) and selected pictures to color (pages 54-64) in this book can be copied to give as handouts.

The enthusiastic gingerbread baker can bake tiny gingerbread cookie animals, boys and girls and trees for use in cottage yards. An idea for a birthday party is to substitute a small gingerbread house or cookie cottage for the traditional birthday cake by placing candles in the yard.

THINGS TO DO ON THE DAY OF THE PARTY OR WORKSHOP:

Make Royal Icing or rebeat icing recipe if it was made a day ahead. (One recipe makes 4 cookie cottages). Color icing as desired and fill parchment cones about half full. Use medium size twister ties to **very tightly** close the icing cones. Reinforce small pointed ends of parchment cones with a small piece of masking or Scotch tape. Do not cut tips open until ready to use. Put filled bags in a flat box, or on a tray; place in a plastic bag and close with a twister tie in order to keep icing soft and moist.

Set up table or tables with a colorful plastic tablecloth. Waxed paper can be used as place mats (this makes cleanup much easier). Arrange the following supplies at each participant's place: cut grahams, bags of candies, bases, paper towels or napkins, a plastic knife and toothpicks. Place small dishes of cereals, pretzels, nuts, raisins, etc. on the tables for sharing.

At one end of the large table, or on a separate table, set up an area with supplies for the demonstration of how to put together a cookie cottage.

Prepare punch or a chilled commercial drink. Water is often requested because it is most quenching. It is best if cups and drinks are put on a separate table away from the construction area.

PARTY OR WORKSHOP (Continued)

ON THE DAY OF THE PARTY OR WORKSHOP

After the participants arrive:

Hand out gingerbread name tags and gingerbread song sheets. Teach the gingerbread songs and have the group sing along. Show the *Gingerbread Land* video, or *The Joy of Gingerbread Housemaking* video (the cookie cottage segment) if available.

If a video are not available give demonstration showing Easy Steps To Make Cookie Cottages (pages 26 - 29). It is important to demonstrate and clearly explain how to hold the icing parchment cone. Stress squeezing from the top of the cone directly under the twister tie. It is not necessary to completely decorate the cottage or yard during the demonstration.

Participants now construct their own cookie cottages. Be sure to have extra graham crackers available in case of breakage and for the building of the many original ideas conceived by the "house builders". Examples: chimneys, lawn chairs, wagons, cars, garages, greenhouses, hot tubs, dog houses, etc.

Additional icing should be available for spreading in the yards (white icing for snow or green icing for grass).

It is a good idea to arrange a special waxed paper covered area (a cookie sheet with sides or a large box lid) for participants to sprinkle chocolate jimmies or other small sprinkles or sugar trims. Recover and reuse collected "sprinkles" from this area.

Put finished cookie cottages into boxes. Give participants hand outs. Smiling countenances are guaranteed to be your honorarium!

Plan 2-1/2 to 3 hours for a party or workshop.

II. Cookie Cottages - Parties and Workshops

PARTY INVITATIONS AND NAME TAGS

Make your own gingerbread party invitations using any of the following ideas: an original gingerbread house drawing or the house illustrated here, copies of cookie cottage pictures (pages 23, 25, or 30) or pictures of gingerbread boy and girl cookies.

Name tags are very helpful for teachers or adult helpers. The children's names can be put on gingerbread boys and girls as pictured below or on the gingerbread house used for the invitation.

34

III. Teachers and Parents Activities for Children

THE GINGERBREAD LADY

III. Teachers and Parents - Activities for Children

A GUIDE TO GINGERBREAD LAND

You can offer children a fun-filled Magical Land of Gingerbread with no baking, icing or candy. Offer the treasures on the following pages to children and their imaginations will do all the rest.

I hope the Anecdotes will inspire you and you can also read them to children.

Reading the Fairy Tale, THE GINGERBREAD QUEST (pages 45-50) to children will provide delightful entertainment and give them an opportunity to put on a play, acting out the story. They may be encouraged to draw and color their own pictures or write their own gingerbread stories.

The Gingerbread Songs (pages 51-53) are "gems" children love to sing over and over and hum while they color, draw or play. These songs are sung by children on the video *Gingerbread Land*.

Consider enlarging the Pictures to Color (pages 54-64) for bulletin boards.

Decorate the Undecorated House (page 59) with items from the Color, Cut and Paste page (page 58) or allow children to arrange the cut-outs in their own original pictures. Other coloring possibilities are the Undecorated House (in Pictures to Color section) and Gingerbread Boy and Girl patterns (pages 122 and 123).

Picture from THE GINGERBREAD HOUSE and CREOLE RESTAURANT
741 - 5th Street, Oakland, CA 94607

III. Teachers and Parents - Activities for Children

ANECDOTES BY THE GINGERBREAD LADY

HOUSE FOR ALL AGES

"...Ida Heistand's summer season gingerbread house was a house to remember. It was her 99th birthday present. She directed its construction like a firm but loving builder - each confection placed squarely and unquestionably in its proper place. There was a gingerbread rocking chair on a carpet of rainbow colored sprinkles inside the house. A candy birthday cake with tiny icing candles on a gingerbread picnic table and coconut strip benches decorated a patio at one end of the house. A garden of cinnamon drop tomatoes, Dynamint cucumbers, gumdrop eggplants, bright orange M&M pumpkins and gumdrop carrots invited a gingerbread Peter Rabbit who ran off with one gumdrop carrot. A gingerbread girl was working in the garden with a pretzel hoe just as Ida had done many times in her real garden.

What a house was made that day! Three generations of loving hands put it together - - Ida, her granddaughter, Phyllis Stroud and great-granddaughters, Tami and Dawn. Nothing was too extravagant. After all, this was Ida's tribute! The gingerbread house stood in a Plexiglas cover, as a centerpiece on Ida's 99th and 100th birthday tables. It symbolized decades of homemaking; of crafting each nook and cranny in her houses, made from brick and mortar, with the same love that this one was crafted in gingerbread, icing and confections. It was very special to Ida that the Gingerbread Lady displayed her house at the Smithsonian Institution."

SEEN AND UNSEEN DELIGHTS

"...When building a gingerbread house, there is an option to furnish the inside before putting on the roof. The furnishings can be simple or elaborate. When my son, John, and daughter, Linda, were children, they always insisted upon a gingerbread Christmas tree surrounded by candy and cookie packages, chairs, tables, lamps, and gingerbread people inside their house. It was fun for their friends to peek through the cut-out windows to discover the doll house-like interior. Cookie cottages and gingerbread houses which do not have cut-out windows can be filled with many surprises. Their furnishings and the confections inside are fun to discover when the houses are being eaten".

III. Teachers and Parents - Activities for Children

ANECDOTES BY THE GINGERBREAD LADY

  ### HALLOWEEN GINGERBREAD

"...Anne Greathouse had wonderful Halloween gingerbread birthday parties. She and her friends created Halloween cookie cottages and large gingerbread houses for centerpieces. They all could have won prizes for their many clever original ideas. White icing covered gingerbread ghosts which came out of chimneys; black icing bats flew along the side of the chimneys and under eves. Gingerbread boys and girls were dressed in Halloween icing costumes. On the back of one house was an icing mouse- hole, and beside it was an icing mouse ready to dart inside. Gingerbread witches, cats, gingerbread boy scarecrows and pumpkin patches were used in the yards. When Anne's mother said, "I think you girls are using too many candy pumpkins." Anne replied, "But it was a good year!" Gingerbread tombstones simulated fantasy cemeteries with edible ghosts, mummies and goblins. Fences of pretzels and colorful candy corn enclosed many of the yards."

III. Teachers and Parents - Activities for Children

ANECDOTES BY THE GINGERBREAD LADY

A FAILURE – A HAPPY MEMORY

"...In one grandmother's first attempt to make cookie cottages with her grandchildren, the icing was not stiff enough, some houses would not stand up and the roofs slipped off others. The children laughed and giggled a lot and they ate the collapsed houses for a dessert feast. Grandma considered the whole experience a fiasco. The grandchildren kept asking when they could make houses again. Their grandma finally agreed. Several weeks later she was very happy that the second house-building party was a success; all the houses stood up and roofs stayed on. She was very puzzled when the "kids" kept saying that the first time they built cookie cottages was the most fun."

Nick Edwards drew this Ranch Style Cookie Cottage for The Gingerbread Lady

A VISIT WITH THE GINGERBREAD LADY

Gingerbread houses are another world of construction; one that doesn't require backhoes, payloaders, dump trucks and cranes, but rather a good imagination and nimble fingers - a project that allows you to be the engineer.

Every time I work on a gingerbread house my sole destiny is to create an original masterpiece that looks and tastes absolutely delicious. I get an inspiration to do the best job I'm capable of doing. Memories of previous triumphs and failures drive me to work. My creativity runs wild while I form the graham crackers into a miniature house. By now my architectural feat has taken a recognizable shape and thoughts and images become real. Suggestions from the gingerbread lady (head foreman) edge me toward completion. After some minor refinements and a finishing touch my work ceases.

Many hours of work pay off, not in money, but in the satisfaction of completing yet another gingerbread original. It's a day that has been unforgettably fun - with a tasteful reward.

John Brislin (age 14)

III. Teachers and Parents - Activities for Children

ANECDOTES BY THE GINGERBREAD LADY

...BY TEACHING YOU'LL BE TAUGHT

"...Children should be encouraged to try out their ideas, even when the teacher isn't sure they will work. The first trains made from graham crackers were created at one of the Gingerbread Lady's workshops. She was so impressed with their originality and success that she asked if she could buy one. Naturally, the creator, Marc Lemon didn't want to part with his masterpiece. Marc did agree to build another train and train station for the Gingerbread Lady to show other children. She was amazed at his knowledge of trains and architectural skills as he crafted trains and stations in graham crackers. A year later Marc won a first prize at the Historic Strasburg Inn Gingerbread House Competition for his spectacular gingerbread train and station."

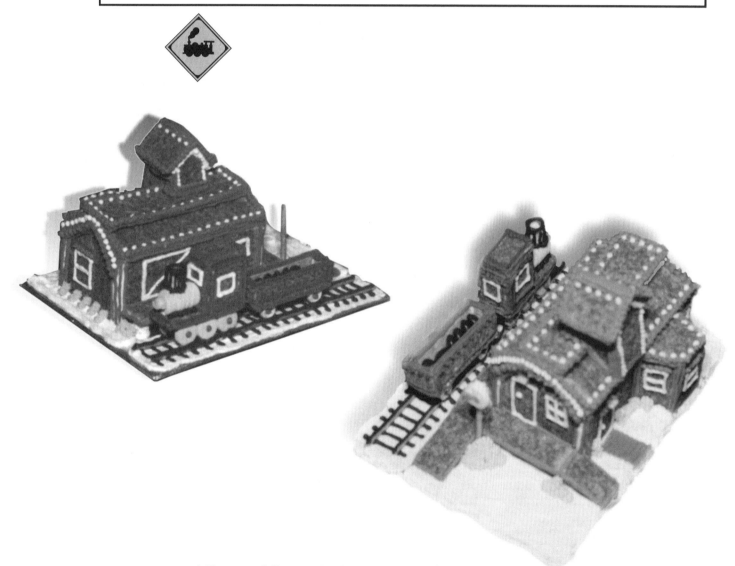

A Train and Station Replica of Marc Lemon's Original "Gram Station"

Home Ec Teacher and Mom "Extraordinaire"

Dixie Heacock, Home Economics teacher at Warwick High School, includes Gingerbread Housemaking in a Family & Consumer Sciences curriculum.

Her Culinary Arts classes have designed and entered local gingerbread competitions They have made An Amusement Park with an amazing Ferris wheel, carrousel and train, a marvelous edible Emerald City including a "ginger-tin-man" and a huge icing hot air balloon to take Dorothy back to Kansas. Their Country Village had a grist mill with a working water wheel (created by using parts of a student's erector set. One year four different scenes depicted a Wooded Cottage in all four seasons of the year. (The same cottage built four times: snow, with bird's nests, green grass and autumn leaves.) Their gingerbread entries brought acclaim to their school by winning a collection of blue ribbons and field trips were taken with prize monies. Plus these students have a skilled craft to carry on as a tradition with their own families.

One boy, who was inspired by Dixie to become a Chef, designed and made an entire gingerbread village. The Gingerbread Lady displayed it at the Smithsonian Institution and later it was on exhibition at a local library.

Dixie's Child Development classes have built houses as part of a preschool program. They have taken their gingerbread workshop "on the road" to Elementary Schools to showing how to make their edible creations.

When students in a spring cooking class were making cookie cottages, the state UGI, home economist came to check the gas appliances. She was so impressed with the houses students were making, she asked Mrs. Heacock, if she would do a program for several hundred Home Ec Teachers in Hershey, PA. "You need The Gingerbread Lady", Dixie told her. Patti was contacted and she and Dixie gave the program together. It was a big success.

Dixie's friends, including Patti Hudson, wear delightful gingerbread sewing projects Dixie has made using gingerbread boy and gingerbread house designs.

Austin and Alex, Dixie's sons, have made a wide variety of gingerbread creations and won prizes in local contests. Their football field and stadium with gummy bear football players and gummy bear fans was a treasure. A Three Little Pigs scene had pink marshmallow pigs and they did a great rendition of The North Pole. Dixie and her boys have put on many gingerbread workshops at their church. Dixie's recipe uses flour, sugar, spices, and includes a lot of smiles, warmth and heart.

Dixie is an inspiration as a Teacher and Mom. She is a Gingerbread Lady in her own right!

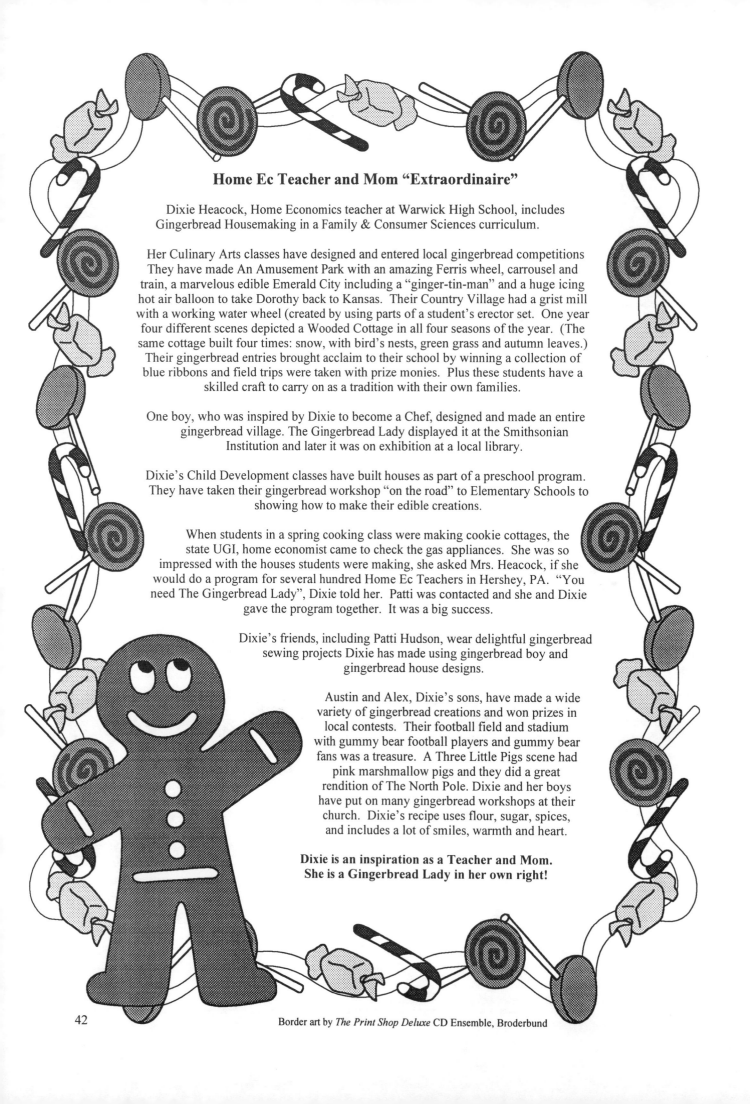

Border art by *The Print Shop Deluxe* CD Ensemble, Broderbund

III. Teachers and Parents - Activities for Children

ANECDOTES BY THE GINGERBREAD LADY

EDIBLE FLOWER GARDENS

"...Children are very inventive in their use of candies, sprinkles and icing when creating flower and vegetable gardens in the yards of their cottages which are often given as gifts to grandparents, teachers or friends. Eight year old, Jill Brislin's beautiful formal colonial flower gardens which she made around her cookie cottage would have impressed even Williamsburg gardeners".

ICING RAINSPOUTS

"...The Gingerbread Lady's neighbor, Tony Roda has made many cookie cottages. On one occasion Tony's house had an outdoor movie theater. The movie screen was a chocolate Andes mint and the audience was gummy bears. Tony created swimming pools, boxing rinks for gummy bears, and the most memorable feature, after he said the words, 'By George, this is going to work!' he had made icing rainspouts."

HIGH TECH / HIGH TOUCH - GINGERBREAD STYLE

"...Pretzels (large and small, sticks and twisted) are often used in many ways on gingerbread houses and cookie cottages. They can be piles of firewood logs, fences, walkways and log cabin walls. Six-year old Seth Bair arranged pretzels on the roof of his house. He put tiny yellow candies between his pretzel solar panels to symbolize captured sunbeams."

RELAX...YOU CAN EAT YOUR MISTAKES

"...The Gingerbread Lady, when instructing children, always makes them laugh by telling them they will be able to eat their mistakes. She explains they don't have to worry if something doesn't work out as they planned, or if they change their mind about an idea midway -- just eat it and do it over -- some mistakes lead to even better ideas. Nibbling or sharing mistakes with others is part of the fun. 'I sure wish I could eat my spelling mistakes', one boy commented in a very serious manner to the Gingerbread Lady."

III. Teachers and Parents - Activities for Children

ANECDOTES BY THE GINGERBREAD LADY

THE UBIQUITOUS GUMMY BEAR

"...Wonderful, versatile additions to cookie cottages and gingerbread houses, gummy bears have been used in many creative ways.

With white icing snow on their paws, many gummy bears have been seen building icing snowmen. Others are skiers with pretzel or licorice skis. Down hills of icing snow, gummy bear sledders practice their sport on sleds of Necco wafers, grahams or Andes mints. They ice skate on frozen candy or icing lakes. One gummy bear climbed up an icing ladder that was leaning against an ice cream cone tree to hang his tree lights. Trudging through snow drifts, colorful bears seek their mail from gumdrop mail boxes. House roofs have been shingled and repaired, chimneys have been built, and TV antennas installed by gummy bears. Some Santa bears have been seen on roofs preparing to go down the chimney, while other bears are on roofs just because they seem to like the view.

Gummy bears have been known to stand three and four on top of one another to peek inside open windows. They dive from diving boards into pools and soak in hot tubs of all sizes built of grahams and filled with blue icing water. There definitely have been gummy bear picnics. Hawaiian theme little grass shack cookie cottages have hula dancing gummy bears in grass skirts with leis on brownulated sugar beaches beside blue icing oceans. Bear surfers ride large icing waves on Necco wafer surf boards chased by candy sharks. Gummy bears have been fishermen, babies in carriages; they have pulled wagons, pushed lawn mowers, played ball, jousted, and been in teams of gardeners. Colorful and versatile bears willingly await all sorts of new fun activities which builders of gingerbread houses can dream up for them."

THE GINGERBREAD QUEST

by

Sheila Audet

Illustrations by Samantha West

Copyright Sheila Audet and Samantha West 1987 - all rights reserved

THE GINGERBREAD QUEST

There once was a land of No Bake.
No one in the land had a cake.
There were squash and peas, meat and flakes...
Apples, raisins and even a date!
But there was no Smell and no Aroma!
Nothing to make you Salivate.
No one knew, of course, that such a thing was a Thing, of course!
Their tastebuds had never experienced the Great Gingerbread Force,
So you may say, so what?
But listen, there has to be Aroma and Smell
And Sweet Gingerbread Baking, somehow!

This little town of No Bake was on a hill beside No Lake.
In No Bake there lived two wonderful beings
Called Green Irene and Yellow Yake.
Who were magically touched one night in mid-December
By the Gingerbread Queen in a wonderful dream.
They awoke in a mist so real they not only could feel it
And smell it, they could almost Taste it!
But what was this wonderful smell beyond description,
That perked their Odorific Syndrone?
Green Irene and Yellow Yake decided upon a Quest
To locate the smell of this wonderful Zest!
They dressed up in coat and glove...and
Followed this magical mist of Smell...
It took one day and one night and a boat across No Lake
To reach the place of delicious Smell and "wonder-full" Taste.
But, Oh, my, my..we're getting ahead of our story, now,
For these two had yet to search
For what made Smell and Taste even work!

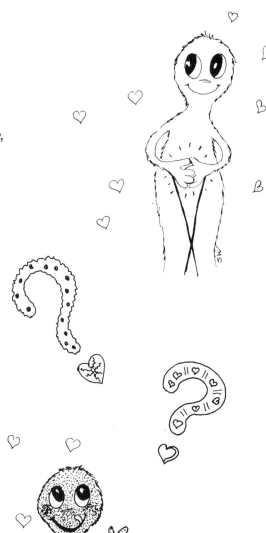

Then before their eyes a house like they'd never seen
Filled the wondering gaze of Yellow and Green.
When they reached the Gate, they were most amazed
At the beautiful Maze before their gaze!
There were candies, jellies, and things galore...
All squooshed with icing to the soft brown walls.
Oh, what Joy! Oh, what Fun!
And their adventure had just begun!
Over the door were the letters: M - Jelly-Bean - M.
What else could that mean but the address of a Gingerbread Queen?!
Oh, the wonderment of this Magical Kingdom!

There suddenly was this rich, deep Voice:
"Who is at my Gingerbread Door?"
You see, of course, this wonderful lady, had been just waiting
For two such Crazies.
"Oh," said Green Irene, "It's only Yellow Yake from No Bake across No Lake."
"Oh," said Yellow Yake, "It's only Green Irene that wants to know about this thing."
"Come ahead, my little ones,
Gingerbread Mouse will lead you on."
Guess what appeared in an instant split?
A Gingerbread Mouse as cute as an itch!

She took them past many beautiful and wonderful things...
Tables of chocolate and lamps of licorice...
Chairs of wondermint and latticed cookies...
Oh, the smell! Oh, the wonder!
And they had a NEED to Eat and Plunder.

***POOF.....!!** There she was, Miss Patti Cake Cakes,*
Dressed in sugar and a pinch of brown spice,
Circled by that Mist of Smell that was ever so nice!
A Gingerbread Lady of great delight!
Her ruffled hat was ever so Neat,
With curls peeping out from just underneath!
Her apron, so crisp, had a smidgen of dough
Symmetrically placed right on its bow!
She was in a spinning whirl
Baking her gingerbread in a feverish swirl.
"Green Irene and Yellow Yake!
You made it safely across No Lake!
In this Land you may eat and you may plunder
For that's why Gingerbread Land's a Wonder.
To fill your stomachs and beg for more..
'Til your tummies bulge! What a delightful Chore!
But I must get back to baking.
Right now, I can speak no more!
There will never be Taste in No Bake
If I never complete this chore."

"Oh, my. Oh, woe!", said Green Irene.
"Oh, what can we do?", said Yellow Yake.
"We would like to help, Miss Patti Cakes,
But we don't know what baking WE can possibly do! Do You?"
"My precious Green Irene and Yellow Yake...
I don't have time now to belly-ache!
But! I have an idea!
My Book could teach you ever so quickly,
How to bake a Gingerbread Cake.
If you will Read you will See
Just how a cake can come to be!
So, quickly turn the pages and learn real fast...
The Way to Start the Gingerbread Quest!
Oh, my Heart! You may rescue me
For it says in the myth that two such as you,
When you get through this Book,
May be the Saviors of the Gingerbread Cook."

Meanwhile back in No Bake across No Lake
Atop the highest peak in reach,
Was Witch No Taste. "I must make haste
And get that Patti Cakes before she bakes too many cakes.
THAT FLAKE! What can I do?
I know! I'll BURN her cakes before it's too late!
I have total control of all schnozzoles
So every good smell will fall under my spell.
She also has Green Irene and
Yellow Yake cooking and baking
Those silly cakes, topped with dates,

That they'll ship in crystal crates across No Lake!
I tell you true, not one smell, not one aroma,
Not one jelly bean, or odor,
Or Gingerbread Flake will pass by my inspection gate.
For, I'm mean old No Taste with schnozzole control
And no Gingerbread cake will EVER bake in No Bake.
I must make haste!"
And so she sped away, top speed,
Upon her broom of doom and gloom, and ugly curly-ques.
"Here I come you Gingerbread Flakes!
I will crumble and tumble
And virtually plunder every cookie and cake,
It will be GINGERBREAD RUE-INN!"

You see, while Miss Patti Cakes became a Baker of Goodness
And Love and Goodwill on top of Gingerbread Hill,
Witch No Taste created a large, invisible Wall
Around No Bake to keep out the smell of all Cake!
But the wonderful Gingerbread Mouse
Had nibbled a hole in that invisible wall
And through it Gingerbread cakes were wafting a Call
To Green Irene and Yellow Yake to save No Bake!

Then Witch No Taste now on her broom
Headed to Gingerbread Hill to perform her tricks
Of Doom and Gloom,
When she suddenly Braked in Mid-broom Flight!
A voice in her ear said, "Stop This flight!
Your Haste will make Waste, No Taste!
You must get the Gingerbread Mouse!
She has nibbled a hole in the invisible wall,
Through it a Gingerbread Smell is pouring.
Right now a small Gingerbread cloud is soaring!
Someone with a schnozzole will soon get a sniff
And try to determine from whence comes that whiff?
You know that is not good!
Mouse will nibble and nibble until that invisible wall
Becomes a mere dribble!
At all costs that Mouse must be stopped
Before your schnozzole control is popped!"
The Witch said, "But how?"
"So far, only Green Irene and Yellow Yake
Have been infected by Miss Patti Cakes.
Kidnap Green Irene on her morning stroll.
Then they will come to fetch her
And you'll have, not only Mouse, but them all!"
The Witch said, "I will perch atop this
Gingerbread Hill and wait for her to appear."

Meanwhile, Green Irene and Yellow Yake were
Just awakening from a Gingerbread Break.
Said Green Irene, "I think I will go pick some
Beautiful holly berries for Miss Patti Cake Cakes."
"OK," said Yellow Yake, "I've learned to bake it,
I know I can make it.
So, be very quiet and let her awake
To somebody else's Gingerbread bake."

*So, off she went in the Crystal Forest
With everything a mirror of Gingerbread Hearts.
Snowflakes were falling like giant sugar lattice works...
Ever so gently upon the earth.
The Crystal Forest had just awakened to chimes and bells
And heavenly smells.
When, suddenly everything went dark and still!
Not one sound. Not one thing moved.
Green Irene was frozen still
In a deep, dark chill!
Then Witch No Taste swooped down
From atop the Hill and swept
Irene off in an instant swirl.*

*Miss Gingerbread Patti Cakes woke up
In a quivering start. She had felt
The whole thing --- mirrored in her Heart of Hearts!
"Quick, Quick!!" she screamed to
Yellow Yake and Gingerbread Mouse.
"We must make haste and save Green Irene
From Witch No Taste."
Yellow Yake said, "Everything is baked!"
"Oh! Aren't you Great, Yellow Yake?!
We are on our way," said Miss Patti Cakes.
She swept up batches of gingerbread cookies
And cakes and goodies galore
Soon her Golden Van's shelves bulged with so much Lore
That wagon could hold not one cookie more!
"Here we come, Witch No Taste!
Your spell is already breaking!
The Gingerbread Force is running its Course."
They went through the Wall and all of a sudden
Every window and door began to fly open!
"Give them a cookie. Give them a cake!
The Spell will be broken the minute they taste!"*

*They soon had an army of Gingerbread followers
Who climbed to the highest peak in reach on top of No Taste.
And Witch No Taste they found - Post Haste!
They pushed and broke down the castle door
In seconds, flat as the floor.
There was the Witch, in puddles of tears.
"You have rue-ined my Land
That I carefully planned!"*

*"Oh, no," said Miss Gingerbread Patti Cakes.
And she extended her hand filled with Gingerbread Cake,
"Just a bite, and you'll See this land will be filled
With Love and Rainbows galore,
Never will spite live here anymore!"*

*Witch No Taste took a bite of Miss Patti Cakes Cake!
Then, in a whisk, the Magic began
And the Gingerbread Force finished its spiraling Course!
Witch No Taste began spinning
In sugary threads of such sweet confection*

That anyone's mouth would have watered in great expectation!
And, when the spinning was spun and the confection was done,
Witch No Taste was now a Radiant One, with a rolling pin wand!
For she had been, you see, Miss Patti Cakes' lost twin,
Who in days long ago had wandered off and fell down
A deep, dark hole.
When she climbed out she had forgotten
The beauty of Smell and Taste
And lived with a horrible Blinding Head-ache!
But this Bite of Gingerbread Gleam
Was just like an Aspirene!
With her headache removed, her memory restored,
Witch No Taste awoke with a quivering start!
Miss Patti Cakes hugged her in a Gingerbread Hug
Witch No Taste became a wonderful Queen of Taste,
As their hearts met and embraced.
The Land now has TWO Radiant Queens
Whose hands blessed everyone, especially Irene!
Now Happiness reigns in the Land of Gingerbread Taste
With Love and Rainbows galore,
For everyone had cake and there no longer is
A Land of No Bake! For these Two Saviors - Green Irene and Yellow Yake -
Were true to the Myth and Miss Patti Cake Cakes!!

POOF!!!!

THE GINGERBREAD QUEST, A Fairy Tale
is dedicated to
KITTY LOVING SHENK
A Mentor, Teacher and Lover of all Tales

Gingerbread Land

words and music by Alisa Bair

1. Col-or-ful can-dies, ic-ing as white as snow. Gin-ger-bread land is where I love to go. It's the land where dreams come true; I can be me, and you can be you. It's the on-ly place where you can eat your mis-takes! I wish the world, I wish the world, I wish the world could be this way.

2. Make a house, or create a family.
   Gingerbread folks are almost like you and me.
   Icing for hair and eyes that twinkle,
   Raisins for buttons on clothes that won't wrinkle.
   It's the only place where you can eat your mistakes!
   I wish the world, I wish the world,
   I wish the world could be this way. (Yum.)

© 1985 by Alisa Bair. All rights reserved. Used by permission.

My Heart's in this House

words and music by Alisa Bair

1. I made a house of sweet de-cor; do you have eyes to see that just be-hind its can-dy door is a smile from me. My heart's in this house, you see. Each one that I make is new when I make it just for you; when I make it just for you.

2. If you will take a look inside
    the window all trimmed with snow,
   You'll see me there, and I'll confide
    you're special to me, as you know.
   My heart's in this house, you see.
    Each one that I make is new
   When I make it just for you,
    when I make it just for you.

© 1986 by Alisa Bair. All rights reserved. Used by permission.

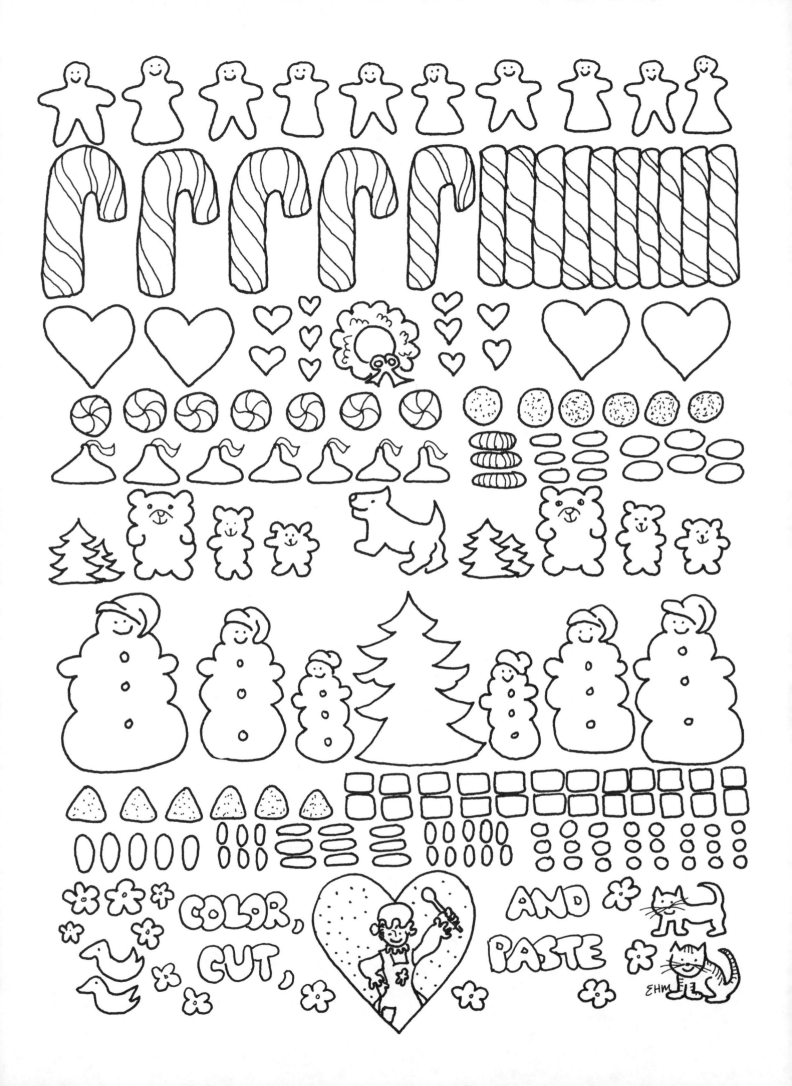

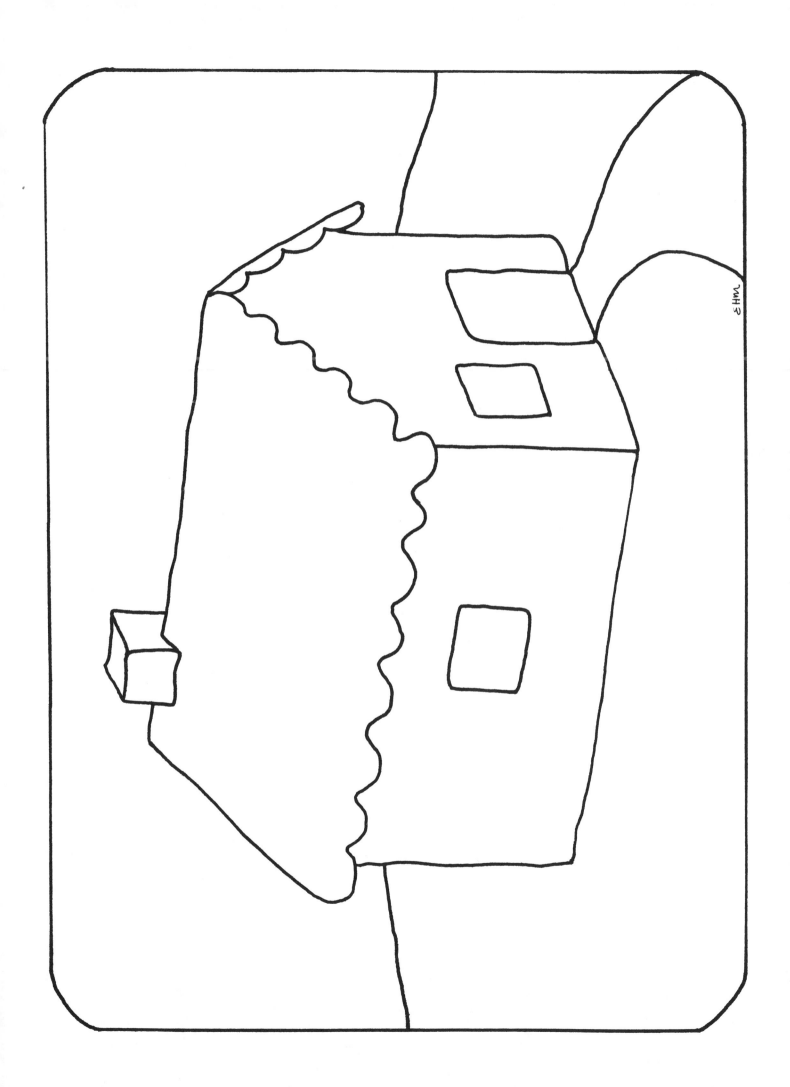

A Victorian Gingerbread House

Plate A

A GINGERBREAD COVERED BRIDGE

Plate B

A BASIC GINGERBREAD HOUSE

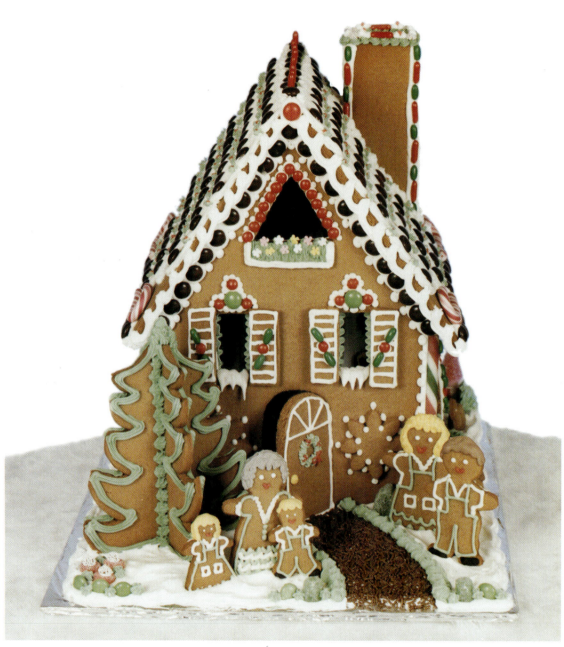

GRANDMA'S GINGERBREAD HOUSE

Plate D

IV. Gingerbread Gift Ideas

IV. Gingerbread Gift Ideas

GIFT IDEAS FOR CHILDREN

DECORATED GINGERBREAD BOY AND GIRL COOKIES - These cookies are always a "hit" with children. Cookie cutters or patterns in this book can be used

A GINGERBREAD COOKIE FAMILY - Use patterns or cookie cutters for a large boy and girl (the mother and father), and a small boy and girl (the children). Cookie cutter dogs and cats can be used to make cookie family pets. Whenever possible, allow children to decorate their own cookies, thus turning the gift into a wonderful creative activity.

A GINGERBREAD HOUSE COOKIE - Use a gingerbread house pattern (Mini-Swiss House, page 94) which makes a small cookie, or use the side (gable end) of the Basic Bungalow house (page 97) which makes a large cookie. (House cookie example page 76). These cookies may be decorated in many ways. Examples: draw with Royal icing a door and window, ice roof edges, add small candies (M&Ms, Snocaps, or cinnamon hots). Children enjoy helping to bake any of the suggested gift cookie ideas and most of all to help decorate these cookies to give to grandparents, teachers or friends. A personal handmade gift is a joy to give and to receive!

GINGERBREAD COOKIE STORYBOOK CHARACTERS - Trace figures from story books onto lightweight cardboard to use as the pattern for the gingerbread cookies. Cookie cutters of some storybook characters are available. Bake cookies to give as gift accompanying the gift of a children's storybook. You will have a thrilled child!

Examples: A gingerbread boy cookie for THE GINGERBREAD BOY
A gingerbread boy and girl cookie and/or a gingerbread house cookie for HANSEL AND GRETEL. A gingerbread boy cookie and/or bear cookie for WINNIE THE POOH.

GINGERBREAD CHRISTMAS TREE ORNAMENT COOKIES - (Pages 68 - 69)

SMALL GINGERBREAD FAVORS - (Page 70). Both of these ideas make excellent gifts for a child or for an entire family. School children can decorate these cookie ideas, and any of the above as a classroom activity to give as gifts to parents or grandparents.

Ideas for Packaging Gingerbread Cookie Gifts - Be sure Royal icing has dried for several hours. Purchase white styrofoam trays from bakeries or make a tray of foil-covered cardboard. Arrange cookies on trays and cover with plastic wrap or put into plastic bags. Tie with colorful yarn or ribbon. When giving cookie characters with storybooks, wrap cookies separately with plastic wrap, then wrap together with plastic wrap to create a "see-thru" package. Add a tie of ribbon or yarn.

IV. Gingerbread Gift Ideas

GIFT IDEAS (Continued)

A COOKIE COTTAGE - A small house made of graham crackers makes a delightful gift for children and adults (pages 25 - 29)

A GINGERBREAD HOUSE - Gingerbread houses, large or small, are very unique and cherished gifts. Pictured below, the Mini-Swiss (page 94) makes a charming gift and several of them can be made from one batch of gingerbread dough. The Heart House (pages 92-93) makes a medium size house. All of the other house patterns in this book make large gingerbread houses. The Gingerbread Barn (page 18 - 19), a Halloween "Haunted" House (page 39), an Easter Theme House, The Wizard of Oz and many other gingerbread scenes can be created to tell a story or accompany a book as a gift.

A GINGERBREAD TREE CENTERPIECE - (Page 69) (Pattern, Page 113).

A GINGERBREAD SLEIGH - (Pages 72-73). (Pattern, Page 120-121)
Either a Tree Centerpiece or a Sleigh given as a gift will thrill a child or a family.

CROCHETED GINGERBREAD BOY - (Pages 74-75). This gingerbread doll is a very lovable gift for children from one to eight years old. Children add clothes.

A FABRIC GINGERBREAD HOUSE - Any of the patterns for large gingerbread houses can be used by the creative seamstress to make a unique, three dimensional gingerbread house in felt or fabric. Many sewing trims and laces simulate the icing and candy decorations on a real gingerbread house. Felt gingerbread boys and girls, and even furniture, can make this fabric gingerbread house a gift to entertain children for hours.

IV. Gingerbread Gift Ideas

GINGERBREAD CHRISTMAS TREE ORNAMENTS

Trace designs for gingerbread ornaments onto light-weight cardboard or heavy brown paper; use as patterns to cut out cookie dough. Using PATTI'S GINGERBREAD recipe (page 78) roll dough to ¼ inch thick and cut around patterns with a knife. (Leave one inch between cookies). Remove excess dough. **BEFORE BAKING** make a hole with a toothpick ¼ inch from the top edge of the cookie. Bake 8 to 10 minutes in a preheated 350° oven. (Touch test the cookie for doneness). After baking, while the cookie is still hot and on the cookie sheet, carefully reopen the hole with a toothpick. Move the toothpick toward the center of the cookie when opening the hole to prevent later breakage. Allow cookies to cool to warm on cookie sheet. Before decorating cookie, insert heavy-duty thread or light-weight string through the hole making a 1 to 2-inch loop and tie. Decorate cookie ornaments on one or both sides with Royal Icing (page 86). Many commercially available cookie cutters can be used to make gingerbread ornaments. (Tiny gingerbread boys and girls, hearts, bells, stars, etc.). Gingerbread ornaments need to be stored in airtight containers or tins until ready to use. They can be frozen, decorated or undecorated, so they can be made well in advance.

IV. Gingerbread Gift Ideas

CHRISTMAS TREE ORNAMENTS (Continued)

IV. Gingerbread Gift Ideas

SMALL GINGERBREAD FAVORS

Gingerbread boy and girl cookie favors are enjoyed by adults and children. Bake gingerbread boy and girl cookies using patterns (page 95), or two to three inch cookie cutters and cut the same number of round, scalloped or rosette shaped cookies. Any gingerbread dough recipes can be used for these cookies. Decorate gingerbread boys and girls with royal icing as desired, allow to dry one to two hours. Ice the round cookies with white royal icing to look like snow. "Glue" with icing a spearmint leaf candy to the back of each girl and boy cookie. Stand them up on the iced cookie. These make charming favors at each individual's place on a holiday table.

Miniature three-dimensional gingerbread cookie trees can be used for table decorations and favors. Bake the gingerbread trees (patterns: page 95 or 97) or use tree-shaped cookie cutters. Two gingerbread tree cookies (one cut in half), and one round cookie are needed to make each favor. Ice a round cookie with royal icing, build the three dimensional tree in the center of the cookie. First, place the whole tree cookie in the center of the iced cookie base. Next, attach with green or white icing, one of the cookie tree halves to one side of the whole tree cookie. Attach the second tree half to the whole tree cookie.

A combined favor can be made using a three dimensional tree and a gingerbread boy and girl. These can be arranged as described above, on a large four inch round cookie.

Foil covered cardboard bases can be substituted for the round cookies specified above. (Two or three inch diameter for the small favors and four inch diameter for the combination favors).

IV. Gingerbread Gift Ideas

GINGERBREAD TREE CENTERPIECE

Mix a batch of PATTI'S GINGERBREAD recipe (page 78). Refrigerate. Make a 10 inch round base of heavy cardboard or use a cardboard cake base and cover with aluminum foil. Trace Gingerbread Tree pattern (page 113) and, if desired, Boy and Girl patterns, below, (family on page 94) on lightweight cardboard. Roll out gingerbread dough on cookie sheets. (Detailed directions are given in Section I, Baking Gingerbread House Parts, page 9). Place pattern on dough. Cut around pattern twice making two trees. Before baking, cut one in half (without separating) on dotted line as shown.

Bake the two gingerbread trees. After baking, re-cut the one in half, leaving tree to cool on baking sheet. Bake eight gingerbread people cookies using cardboard patterns or family cookie cutters. Make a batch of royal icing (Page 86)

To assemble centerpiece ice the foil covered base with white royal icing to look like snow. Place the whole tree cookie in the center of the iced base. Using green or white icing, attach a tree half to the each side of the whole tree cookie. The tree can be decorated with icing and/or candies. Arrange the people cookies in a circle around the tree facing out. Four can lean against tree branches. The other four can be stood, supported by candy spearmint leaves, iced and placed behind them. People cookies can be decorated ahead of time and should be allowed to dry before arranging them around the tree. Alternatively, they can be decorated after they are placed around the tree.

IV. Gingerbread Gift Ideas

GINGERBREAD SLEIGH CENTERPIECE

BAKING THE SLEIGH

Roll out 1/3 of PATTI'S GINGERBREAD recipe (page 78) directly on a cookie sheet, ¼ inch thick. Place sleigh side pattern (pages 120-121) on dough; cut around edges with a knife; remove extra dough to use again. Bake in preheated 350° oven for 12 to 15 minutes. Cool until warm on the cookie sheet. While the first side bakes, roll out the second 1/3 of dough on a cookie sheet. Turn the sleigh pattern over to cut out the second sleigh side or you will have two right sides. Cut around pattern as before and bake. Roll out the final 1/3 of dough on a cookie sheet. This will be for the bottom, back, and front patterns of the sleigh. These three pieces can be cut out side by side as one large piece; cut along patterns' edges with knife before baking; cut again while hot as soon as removed from the oven. Also trim, while hot, any crooked baked edges to make each piece edge straight. This will assure easy assembly of the sleigh.

Roll out left-over dough on a cookie sheet and cut out gingerbread boys and girls, trees or other designs with cookie cutters or patterns in this book. Remove extra dough to use again.

ASSEMBLING THE SLEIGH

Assemble sleigh on a foil covered, heavy cardboard base (9 x 11 inches), or on a tray, large glass plate, or cutting board. Attach bottom of sleigh to base with Royal Icing (page 86). Apply a generous amount of icing around all edges of bottom piece. Place front and back sleigh pieces into the icing; support them with jars or cans. Apply icing along the two edges of both front and back sleigh pieces. Apply icing along bottom edge of one sleigh side, center it, and press in place against iced edges of front and back pieces, right side out. Repeat with second sleigh side. Support all four sides of the sleigh and allow icing to dry thoroughly for several hours or overnight.

Option: The gingerbread sleigh can be constructed around a small box of cardboard or thin, white Styrofoam (6 inches long x 5½ inches wide x 1½ inches high). The gingerbread sleigh pieces are glued with icing to this box. The sleigh bottom piece can be eliminated or cut ¼ inch smaller on all sides and glued with icing inside the box. This makes a stronger sleigh and is recommended if the sleigh is to be used on a number of occasions or for more than one season.

IV. Gingerbread Gift Ideas

SLEIGH CENTERPIECE (Continued)

DECORATING THE SLEIGH

Make designs on sleigh sides with icing and colored candies (Sno-Caps, cinnamon hots and dark green Dynamints). Two large candy canes can be glued in place with icing as sleigh runners. Gingerbread cookies can be decorated with left over icing

FILLING THE SLEIGH

Fill the gingerbread sleigh with cookies; decorated gingerbread boys and girls and other designs baked from the leftover dough. This centerpiece can be used a number of times by refilling it with your favorite Christmas cookies. If cookies are in short supply, popcorn or dry cereal can be used to fill the bottom of the sleigh while placing cookies on top. The sleigh looks best when very full. Candy canes or candy sticks can be arranged with the cookies. Small square cookies can be decorated to look like packages. The sleigh and gingerbread cookies can be used for a number of seasons if properly stored. To store, place the empty sleigh in a box and seal in a plastic bag closed with a tie. Store in a cool place. If keeping cookies, store them separately in a tin or box in a plastic bag.

IV. Gingerbread Gift Ideas

CROCHETED GINGERBREAD BOY PATTERN

This pattern makes a gingerbread boy 15 inches tall. It requires about 180 yards of brown, and a small amount of white, heavy rug yarn; crochet hook size I; large eye needle; and filling material.

ABBREVIATIONS:

    st = stitch
    ch = chain
    sc = single crochet
    sl st = slip stitch
    tog = together
    dec = decrease
    inc = increase

GAUGE: 3 sts = one inch

PATTERN

BACK
Left Leg: Beginning at lower edge with brown, ch 9.
Row 1: sc in second ch from hook and in each ch to end - 8 sc.
Rows 2 and 3: ch 1, turn, sc in each sc.
Row 4: ch 1, turn, sc across, dec 1 st over last 2 sts.
Row 5: ch 1, turn, dec 1 st over first 2 sts, sc across.
Rows 6 through 12: ch 1, turn, sc across - 6 sc.
Row 13: ch 1, turn, inc 1 st in first st, sc across. Fasten off.

Right Leg: Same as left leg through row 3.
Work decs in rows 4 and 5 at opposite edge of work.
Work same as left leg through row 12.
On row 13, ch 1, turn, sc across, inc 1 st in last st, do not fasten off.

Body - Joining Row 1: ch 1, turn, sc across 7 sts of right leg, ch 3, sc across 7 sts of left leg.
Row 2: ch 1, turn, sc across 7 sts, sc in each ch st, sc across 7 sts - 17 sc.
Row 3: ch 1, turn, sc across.
Row 4: ch 1, turn, inc 1 st each end, sc across.
Rows 5 through 13: ch 1, turn, sc across - 19 sc.

CROCHETED PATTERN (Continued)

Arms - Row 1: ch 1, turn, sc across 19 sts, ch 12 for one arm, turn.
Row 2: sc in second ch from hook, sc in next 10 ch, sc across 19 sc, ch 12 for other arm, turn.
Row 3: sc in second ch from hook, sc in next 10 ch, sc across 30 sc.
Rows 4 through 8: ch 1, turn, sc across - 41 sc.
Row 9: ch 1, turn, sc across 26 sts, do not work last 15 sts.
Row 10: ch 1, turn, sc across 11 sts for neck, do not work last 15 sts.

Head - Row 1: ch 1, turn, inc 1 st each end, sc across - 13 sc.
Row 2: ch 1, turn, sc across.
Repeat last 2 rows twice.
Rows 7, 8: ch 1, turn, sc across - 17 sc.
Row 9: ch 1, turn, dec 1 st each end, sc across.
Row 10: ch 1, turn, sc across.
Repeat last 2 rows twice, then repeat row 9 once more. Fasten off.

FRONT - Same as back.

FINISHING -
Eyes: (Make 2) With white, ch 2, 7 sc in second ch from hook, sl st in first sc. Fasten off, leaving 12-inch length of yarn to sew eyes to face. Embroider mouth as shown with white (add nose if desired).

Beginning at left underarm with wrong sides together, with white sc front and back together around outside, inserting filling before completion, join with sl st in first sc. Fasten off.

Grandma (Mildred S. Hudson) increased this pattern size. She made very large Mr. and Mrs. Gingerbread and a medium size big brother. She made many small boys creating a much loved Gingerbread Family which accompanied The Gingerbread Lady in her travels and they appear on two gingerbread videos.

IV. Gingerbread Gift Ideas

GINGERBREAD HOUSE COOKIE

Border art by *The Print Shop Deluxe* CD Ensemble, Broderbund

V. Recipes

V. Recipes

♥ PATTI'S GINGERBREAD ♥

THIS RECIPE IS FOR MAKING HOUSES AND ORNAMENTS

1 cup vegetable shortening
¾ cup granulated sugar
1 cup molasses (dark or light)
1 teaspoon vanilla
4½ to 5 cups all-purpose flour
    (sift before measuring)
1 teaspoon baking soda
1 teaspoon salt
1 teaspoon cinnamon
2 teaspoons ginger

Cream shortening and sugar in a large mixing bowl with electric mixer until fluffy

Add molasses and vanilla. Mix well.

Sift and measure flour.

Add soda, salt and spices to one cup of flour and sift together.

Add this cup of sifted dry ingredients to creamed mixture. Mix well.

Gradually add remaining flour (about 1 cup at a time), mixing well after each addition. The last cup or ½ cup of flour may have to be worked into the dough using your hands. The dough needs to be stiff but workable, not dry or crumbly.

Divide dough in half, shaping into two rectangles. Wrap in waxed paper or plastic wrap; place in plastic bags and refrigerate 1 to 2 hours or chill overnight. Dough can be kept several days in the refrigerator or up to several months in the freezer. Frozen dough is best thawed overnight in the refrigerator before rolling out to bake.

Roll out dough directly on cookie sheets; cut out house parts or cookies. Bake in preheated 350° oven. Pages 9 and 10 give detailed directions for rolling out and baking the dough to make gingerbread house parts.

This recipe makes one basic gingerbread house (pages 95-97, also, Color Plate C). The large Swiss house (pages 98-101) requires two batches of dough.

TINA STREPKO'S GINGERBREAD

THIS RECIPE IS USED

FOR MAKING HOUSES

6¾ cups flour
1 Tablespoon cinnamon
1½ teaspoon ginger
½ teaspoon salt

1½ cups light corn syrup
1¼ cups brown sugar, packed
1 cup butter or margarine

Stir together in a large bowl
the first four ingredients
(flour, cinnamon, ginger, and salt).

Combine in 2-quart saucepan the remaining three ingredients (corn syrup, brown sugar, and butter or margarine). Cook, stirring constantly, until butter is melted. Remove from heat; stir into flour mixture until well blended.
Refrigerate until dough is cooled to room temperature and easy to handle.
(If it is too cold it is hard to roll out).

Roll out pieces of dough on sheets of foil; then place foil on cookie sheet to bake. Bake in a preheated 350° oven until lightly browned and firm when lightly touched. Thicker pieces may take 20 to 30 minutes to bake; thinner pieces only 12 to 15 minutes. Remove foil sheets to cooling rack. Cool completely before removing foil.

NOTE: Before gingerbread has cooled, check size of pieces by placing patterns on them. Trim to size as necessary.

> "...Tina Strepko, from Ephrata, Pennsylvania, is an award winning builder of gingerbread houses. She won BEST OF SHOW three times at The Historic Strasburg Inn Gingerbread House Contest. She created a Victorian Governor's Mansion, a replica of The Washington House at Historic Strasburg, and an authentic replica of an existing Pennsylvania covered bridge complete with an Amish horse and buggy. Her gorgeous two-story Victorian Doll House took first place, best-in-category, at Peddler's Village Gingerbread House Competition. It also received first place in the Good Housekeeping National Gingerbread House contest."

V. RECIPES

WHOLE WHEAT GINGERBREAD

THIS RECIPE IS FOR MAKING HOUSES OR COOKIES

1 cup molasses
1 cup brown sugar
1 cup margarine
    (2 sticks cut into pieces)
1 egg
6 cups whole wheat flour
    (pastry if available)

1¼ teaspoons salt
¾ teaspoon baking soda
1¼ teaspoons baking powder
4 teaspoons ginger
1¼ teaspoons cinnamon
¼ teaspoon cloves

Mix together molasses, brown sugar and margarine in a large pan. Heat while stirring until mixture starts to boil. Remove from heat immediately; set aside to cool.

Measure flour into a large bowl. Put 1 cup of flour into sifter; add salt, soda, baking powder and spices. Stir together and sift into bowl with the other 5 cups flour. Stir all dry ingredients together to distribute evenly.

When molasses mixture is just barely warm, add the egg and mix in thoroughly.

Make a well in the flour; pour all the molasses mixture into the flour at once. Stir together, mixing in all the flour. It will be a very stiff mixture. Knead dough by hand for several minutes on a lightly floured surface or on floured waxed paper. Form dough into 2 or 4 rectangles; wrap in waxed paper or plastic wrap. Set aside at room temperature for 1 to 3 hours. (If kept longer than 3 hours, refrigerate). If dough is refrigerated, set it out for 1 to 2 hours to bring it to room temperature to make the dough easier to roll out.

Roll out the dough on lightly greased cookie sheets. Cut out house patterns, desired designs or cookies.

Bake in preheated 350° oven for 8 to 15 minutes, depending upon size of pieces. It will test done when finger touch no longer leaves an impression on baked cookie dough.

NOTE: THIS RECIPE IS PERISHABLE. FREEZE HOUSES OR COOKIES IF THEY WILL NOT BE EATEN WITHIN TWO WEEKS.

V. Recipes

"DELICIOUS NUTRITIOUS" GINGERBREAD

THIS RECIPE IS FOR MAKING HOUSES OR COOKIES

5 cups whole wheat pastry flour
1 cup soy flour
2 teaspoons soda
4 teaspoons ginger
2 teaspoons allspice
2 teaspoons cinnamon
½ teaspoon nutmeg (optional)
1 teaspoon cloves (optional)

2 teaspoons grated orange or lemon rind
2/3 cup melted butter or oil
2 eggs
½ cup molasses
½ cup honey
¼ cup warm water

Combine dry ingredients in a large bowl and mix together well.

In a second large bowl beat the eggs; add the molasses and honey, continuing to beat while adding the cooled, melted butter or oil and warm water.

Mix in the grated orange or lemon rind.

Gradually add all the dry ingredients to the wet mixture. Mix only until there is no evidence of flour.

Divide dough into 2 or 3 portions; wrap in waxed paper or plastic wrap, and refrigerate several hours or overnight.

Roll out chilled dough between waxed paper, or on baking parchment paper cut to the size of the cookie sheets (bake right on the parchment paper). Cut out desired shapes with cookie cutters or patterns. Remove excess dough.

Bake in a preheated 350° oven for 8 to 12 minutes, depending on the size of the cookies.

TWO BATCHES of dough are required to make a basic gingerbread house (pages 95 - 97).

NOTE: The Sugarless Cream Cheese recipe (page 87) is recommended for constructing "natural" houses or decorating cookies made with this recipe.

THIS RECIPE IS PERISHABLE. FREEZE HOUSES OR COOKIES IF THEY WILL NOT BE EATEN WITHIN A WEEK.

V. Recipes

GINGERBREAD BOY COOKIE TREATS

THIS RECIPE IS FOR MAKING COOKIES

1 cup margarine (softened)	2 tablespoons vinegar
1 cup sugar	6½ cups flour
½ teaspoon salt	1½ teaspoons baking soda
2 eggs	4 teaspoons ginger
1 cup molasses	1 teaspoon cinnamon

Cream margarine, sugar and salt in a large bowl.
Add eggs one at a time, beating well. Add molasses and vinegar; mix in well.

Sift together flour, soda, ginger and cinnamon.
Gradually add dry ingredients to molasses mixture and mix well.
Chill dough 3 to 4 hours or overnight.

Roll out dough between two pieces of waxed paper or directly on greased cookie sheets. Roll to slightly less than ¼ inch thickness. Cut around patterns or use cookie cutters dipped in flour. Combine dough scraps for additional cookies. Chill before rolling out again.
Bake in preheated 375° oven 9 to 10 minutes.
Cool on cookie sheet a few minutes before removing to wire rack.

NOTE: This recipe will make 12 to 13 large gingerbread boys or girls (Patterns pages 122, 123, 125).
FREEZE COOKIES IF THEY ARE NOT TO BE EATEN WITHIN A WEEK.

V. Recipes

STAINED GLASS COOKIES
and Windows

Jeffrey Dow shared these directions
with the Gingerbread Lady

Sort hard transparent candy such as Life Savers or lollipops by color and place in separate small plastic bags. Crush the candy into small, thin pieces (still large enough to pick up). Place each bag on a cutting board. Hit several medium hard times with the flat side of a wooden spoon or roll with rolling pin.

Choose a favorite refrigerator cookie dough recipe. Roll pieces of mixed cookie dough into long, thin, rounded strips.

On a cookie sheet covered with aluminum foil, shape the strips of dough into the outlined shape desired. Join the strips by pressing the ends together. At the top make a loop for hanging.

HALF BAKE the cookie designs in a preheated oven according to chosen dough recipe. Bake 5 - 8 minutes.

<u>Safety tip</u>: Let cookie sheet cool.

Add colored candy pieces to cookie designs. Fill each outline with a thin, even layer of colored candy pieces. do not use different colors in the same space unless you want them to run together.

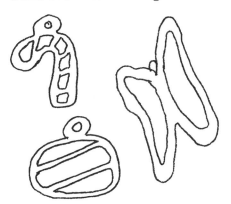

Continue baking cookies – Bake until the candy melts and begins to bubble. This takes about 5 to 8 minutes. Baking time will vary with the size and shape of the cookie

Allow cookies to cool on cookie sheet. When candy hardens, aluminum foil can be peeled from the back of the cookies.

Put strings through the loops at the tops and the stained glass cookies are ready for hanging.

For stained glass window effect in a gingerbread house or church: remove dough from window openings before baking and follow above directions when wall is HALF BAKED.

(The gingerbread recipe on page 79 is recommended – windows may need trimmed to exact shape, after HALF BAKING, before adding candy pieces).

V. Recipes

"PEPPARKAOR" (SWEDISH GINGERSNAPS)

THIS RECIPE IS FOR MAKING COOKIES

5 cups all purpose flour
1 tablespoon ground cloves
1 tablespoon ginger
1 tablespoon cinnamon
1½ teaspoons ground cardamom

½ pound softened butter
1½ cups granulated sugar
¾ cup water
1 tablespoon dark corn syrup
1½ teaspoon baking soda

Measure flour. Combine butter and sugar in a large mixing bowl. Mix together water, spices, soda and corn syrup in a medium size saucepan; bring to a boil.

Pour hot mixture over butter and sugar. Stir until sugar is dissolved and butter melted. Add flour one cup at a time, blending well after each addition.

Refrigerate overnight, storing well covered.
Dough may be kept up to two weeks if refrigerated.

Roll out a small amount at a time of chilled dough to 1/8 inch thick on a lightly floured surface. Cut out cookie designs. Place on an ungreased cookie sheet. (Make a small hole in each cookie with a toothpick if cookies are to be used as hanging decorations).

Bake in a preheated oven at 375° for 6 to 7 minutes or until lightly browned.
Reopen small holes in hot cookies with a toothpick.
Allow cookies to cool before removing from cookie sheets.

Recipe makes about twelve dozen small cookies or six dozen large cookies. If cookies will be used as hanging decorations, insert string through holes before decorating. Decorate with Royal icing (page 86)

"...Thanks to Susan Doyle for sharing this family recipe. Susan makes her cookies in large heart shapes and writes on them the names of children who she knows will be visiting during the holidays. They find their own special cookie on the Christmas tree. They have a choice of taking it home for their own tree or eating it on the spot --- Susan says it is never much of a choice!"

V. Recipes

GINGERBREAD BOY COOKIES

THIS RECIPE IS FOR MAKING COOKIES BY PROFESSIONAL BAKERS

5 pounds granulated sugar
5 pounds brown sugar
14 pounds butter
2 quarts molasses
14 pounds cake flour
14 pounds pastry flour
4 tablespoons baking soda

16 ounces ginger
2 ounces nutmeg
2 ounces cinnamon
½ ounce allspice
½ clove
16 whole eggs

Mix in 60 quart bowl using a paddle type beater.

Cream first three ingredients (sugar and butter).

Sift together all dry ingredients.

Add molasses to creamed butter and sugar mixture

Add eggs to the molasses, butter and sugar mixture. Add gradually being careful not to bread the emulsion. (A small amount of flour may be added if necessary).

Add sifted dry ingredients. Do not overwork the dough.

Refrigerate and allow dough to rest overnight.
This dough can be put through a sheeter.

Stamp out cookie patterns.

Bake at 375° for 10 - 12 minutes in a rack oven.

Yields 220 eight to ten inch boy cookies.

Use raisins for eyes, mouths and buttons or ice creatively.

> Mike Williams, pastry chef for Brauns Caterers, Chillum, Maryland developed this recipe from The Gingerbread Lady's recipes. He baked over a thousand gingerbread boys from this recipe for A Capital Collection in Washington, D.C.

V. Recipes

DECORATIVE ICING RECIPE

THIS RECIPE IS FOR BUILDING AND DECORATING HOUSES AND COOKIES

ROYAL ICING WITH MERINGUE POWDER*

1 pound powdered sugar (not sifted)
3 tablespoons meringue powder**
¼ teaspoon cream of tartar
½ cup minus 1 tablespoon hot tap water

Mix meringue powder with sugar in mixing bowl and add cream of tartar.
Add hot water.
Beat 3 to 4 minutes at low speed with electric mixer until no lumps remain.
Scrape bowl. Beat 5 to 8 minutes on high speed until icing holds stiff peaks.
Keep icing portions covered that are not being used; it dries very quickly.

Doubling the recipe is recommended only if using a heavy-duty mixer.

Refrigerate leftover icing in an airtight container. This icing can be re-beaten to its original stiffness. If made a day ahead, re-beat to stiff peaks before using.

To decorate cookies, gingerbread ornaments; to make snow or icicles
add ¼ to ½ teaspoon water to ½ cup icing.

1 recipe makes 4 cookie cottages. 2 recipes make one basic gingerbread house.
(pages 95-97, also, see Color Plate C).

> ***The U.S. Department of Agriculture and PENN STATE EXTENSION SERVICE do not recommend any icing recipe using raw egg whites (without cooking) because of the possibility of the presence of harmful bacteria.**

> ** ¾ ounce of meringue powder equals 3 tablespoons.
> 1½ ounces (6 tablespoons) will make two (1 pound) recipes.
> 3 ounces (12 tablespoons) will make four (1 pound) recipes.
> Meringue powder can be obtained from cake decorating shops, bakeries or by mail order from food specialty catalogs.

V. Recipes

SUGARLESS CREAM CHEESE ICING

RECIPE IS FOR BUILDING AND THIS DECORATING HOUSES AND COOKIES

16 ounces cream cheese softened
    (room temperature)
2 to 3 teaspoons lemon juice
4 tablespoons honey
2 teaspoons vanilla

Beat cream cheese until creamy.

Gradually add lemon juice, honey and vanilla. Beat well*

For a softer or creamier icing, add a teaspoon at a time of milk or yogurt, beating well after each addition.

Food colors may be added as desired.

*This consistency is perfect for putting together a "natural" whole wheat gingerbread house, or for decorating "delicious nutritious" cookies (page 79).

NOTE: A gingerbread house put together with this icing should be supported with thin Styrofoam or foil covered cardboard. Since it must be refrigerated, the gingerbread will absorb moisture in several hours and become soft. It is best to put this house together just a few hours before it is to be used. This icing will take on a dark color from the gingerbread if refrigerated for more than 8 hours.

V. Recipes

Modeling Candy "Clay"
(Based On a Wilton Recipe)

Confectionery coatings (such as Wilton's Candy Melts) (Mail Order, Page 126) These come in a variety of colors light and Dark chocolate (brown) white, red, yellow, green, blue, and pastels.

1/3 cup light corn syrup

Melt 14 ounces confectionery coatings in top of double boiler or microwave.

Add corn syrup and stir to blend.

Turn mixture out onto waxed paper and let set at room temperature to dry.

Wrap well and store at room temperature until needed.

Modeling candy handles best if hardened overnight.
It can be tinted using paste food-colors. (Knead in color until well blended).

When modeling candy (it will be very hard at first) knead a small portion at a time until workable. If it gets too soft, set aside at room temperature or refrigerate briefly. It can also be rolled out. When rolling out, sprinkle work surface with cornstarch to prevent sticking; roll to about 1/8-inch thickness. To use, the soft "clay" will stick to baked gingerbread or can be attached with frosting dots.

Prepared modeling candy can be stored for several weeks at room temperature in a well-sealed container.

V. Recipes

MASHED POTATO CANDY

1 cup warm unseasoned mashed potatoes
½ teaspoon salt
2 teaspoons vanilla
2 pounds confectioners' sugar

Combine potatoes, salt and vanilla in a large, 4-quart mixing bowl.

Sift confectioner's sugar over potatoes, stirring and adding about one cup at a time. The mixture will liquefy when first sugar is added, then it gradually will begin to thicken. When it becomes the consistency of stiff dough, knead it even if all the sugar has not been added. Sometimes, depending upon the amount of water in the potatoes, more sugar must be added. The consistency should be of a stiff dough so it can be kneaded.

After kneading, cover with a damp cloth; chill until it can be shaped, rolled, or patted into shapes desired. This recipe makes about 8 dozen ½" balls. Candy balls can be decorated with nut pieces. Potato candy can be rolled out on waxed paper; spread with peanut butter, rolled up like a jelly-roll; then cut into slices.

Tina Strepko (page 79) used ten batches of Mashed Potato Candy for the snow landscaping on her prize winning Gingerbread Covered Bridge. She used the Modeling Candy "Clay" to make interior hand modeled accessories in her national award winning Gingerbread Doll House.

V. Recipes

CINNAMON CUT-OUTS
(Non-Edible Fragrant Spicy Ornaments)

6 tablespoons warm applesauce
10 tablespoons cinnamon

Mix together, 6 tablespoons warm applesauce and 10 tablespoons cinnamon to form a ball.

Sprinkle cutting board and rolling pin with cinnamon and roll out dough to ¼ inch thickness.

Use cookie cutters or patterns to make cut-out designs.

Make holes in ornaments with a pencil or a nail.

Place cut-outs on cake rack in 150° oven. Leave oven door ajar. Dry for six hours.

This recipe makes five, two inch gingerbread boy cut-outs or eight to ten, one inch cut-outs.

"...Darby says his Mom has 'Gingermania'. Dottie Papez has taught cookie cottage-making at Darby's and Daniel's school; has given gingerbread birthday parties for nieces, Chris and Heather and for many other children. She sews beautifully! She has decorated aprons, purses and sweaters with gingerbread boys and gingerbread houses. The Cinnamon Cut-outs recipe was given to Gingerbread Lady Patti by Gingerbread Lady Dottie."

VI. Patterns

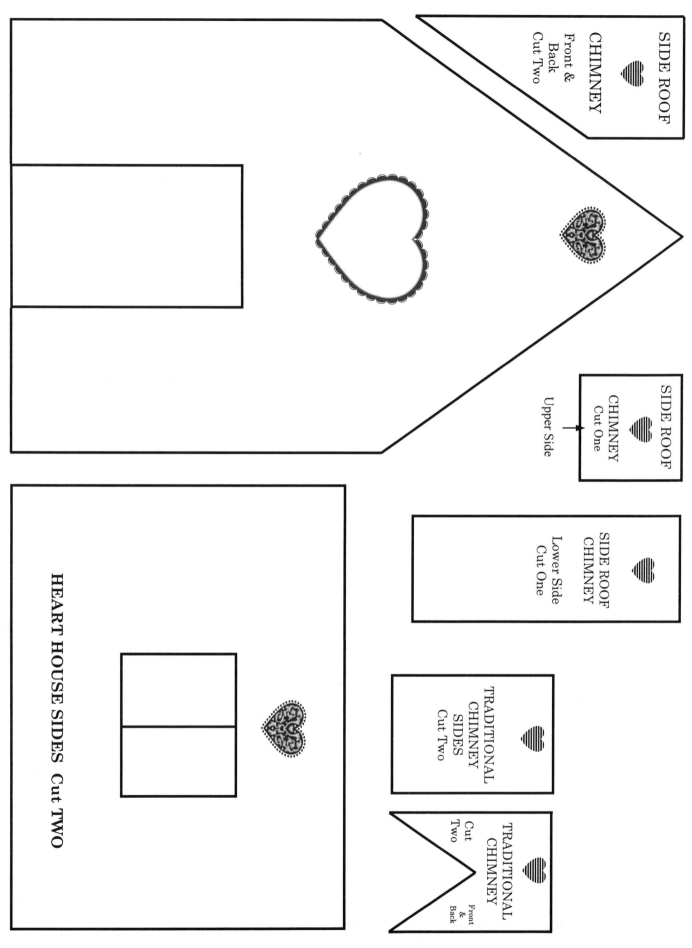

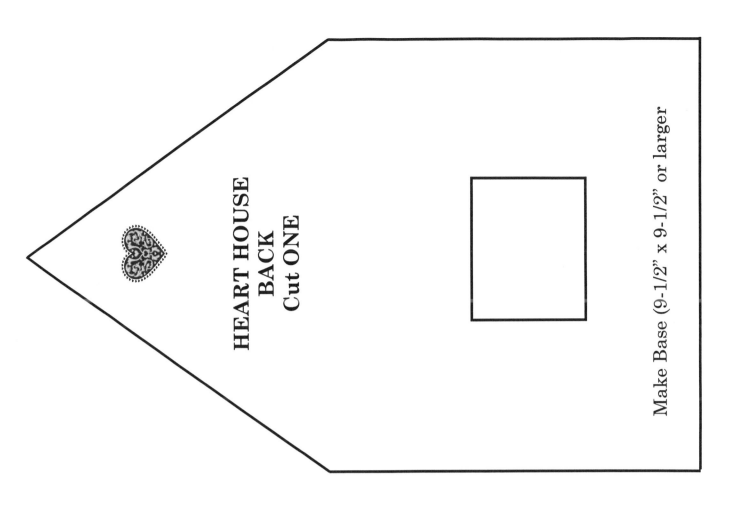

HEART HOUSE BACK Cut ONE

Make Base (9-1/2" x 9-1/2" or larger

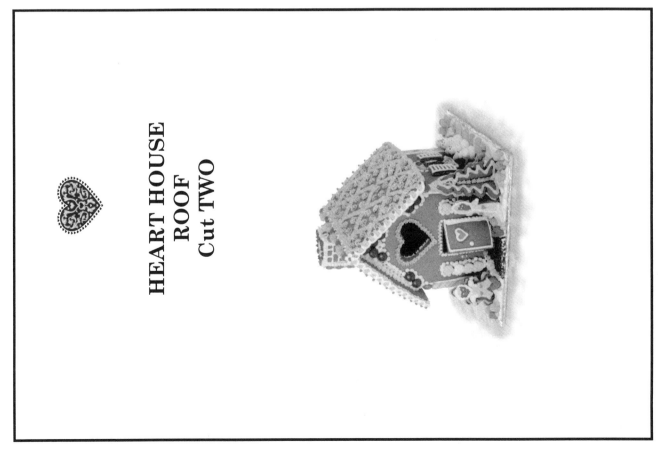

HEART HOUSE ROOF Cut TWO

MINI SWISS HOUSE

SIDE

Cut TWO

MINI SWISS GINGERBREAD HOUSE ROOF

Cut TWO

MINI SWISS HOUSE FRONT & BACK Cut TWO

Door Size Optional

Chimney Front

Chimney Side

Chimney Side

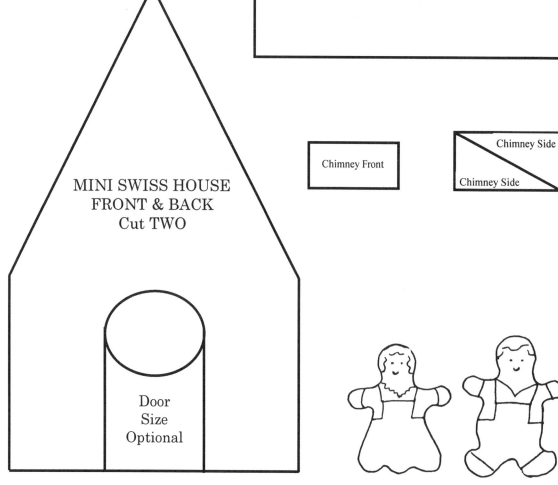

BASIC GINGERBREAD HOUSE ROOF

Cut TWO

See a color picture of this Basic Gingerbread House On Color Plate C.

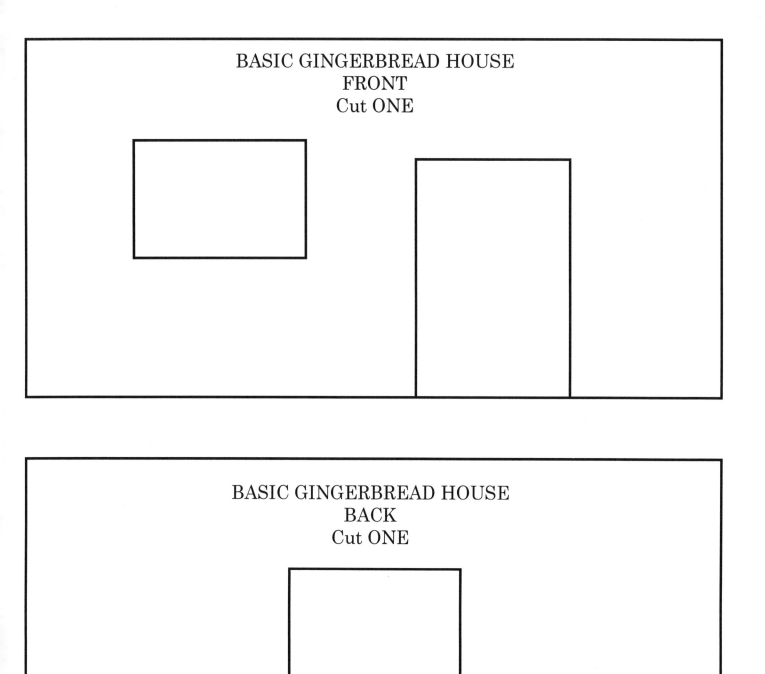

Make Base for this Gingerbreaad House 11' x 15' or 12" x 16"

96

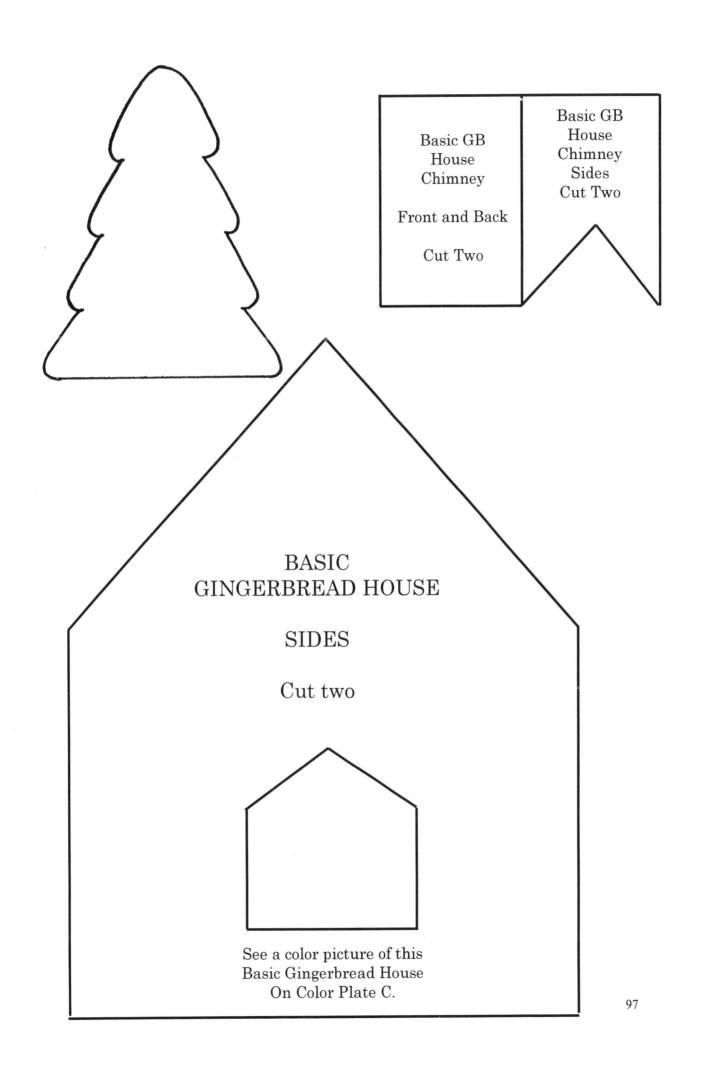

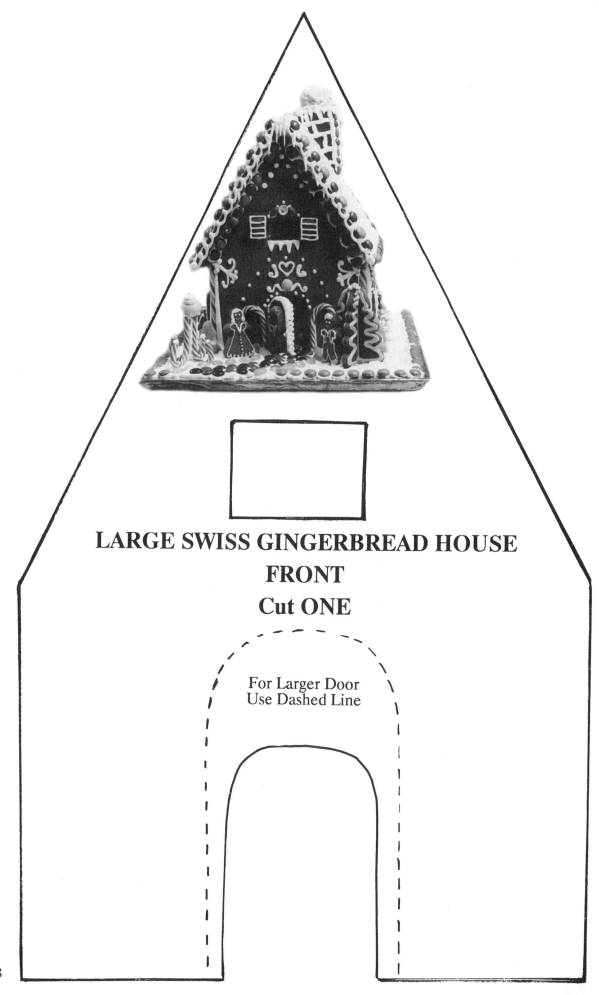

LARGE SWISS GINGERBREAD HOUSE
FRONT
Cut ONE

For Larger Door
Use Dashed Line

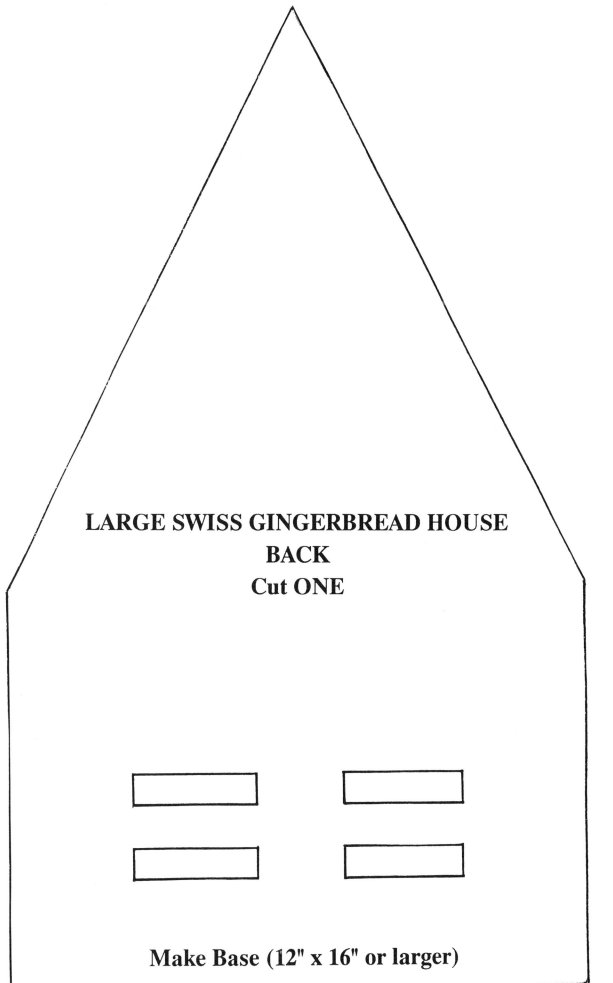

FRONT ↕ BACK

LARGE SWISS GINGERBREAD HOUSE
ROOF
Cut TWO

ROOF TOP

Lg Swiss Chim. Cut 1 Upper Side

LARGE SWISS CHIMNEY

Front & Back Cut TWO

Turn over to cut 2nd piece

LARGE SWISS CHIMNEY LOWER SIDE Cut ONE

LARGE SWISS GINGERBREAD HOUSE SIDES Cut TWO

Bottom

Grandma's House
Chimney
Lower Side
Cut One

Grandma's House Chimney
Front & Back
Cut Two

Turn over to Cut 2nd piece

Grandma's House Front
Window Shutters
Cut four

GRANDMA'S HOUSE

Grandma's House Chimney
Upper Side
Cut One

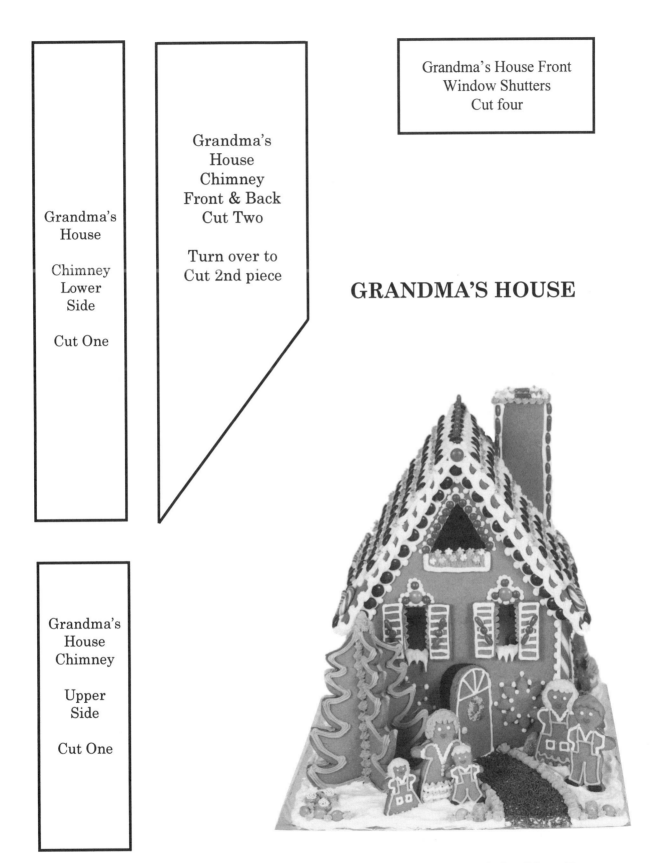

See a color picture of Grandma's Gingerbread House on Color Plate D

103

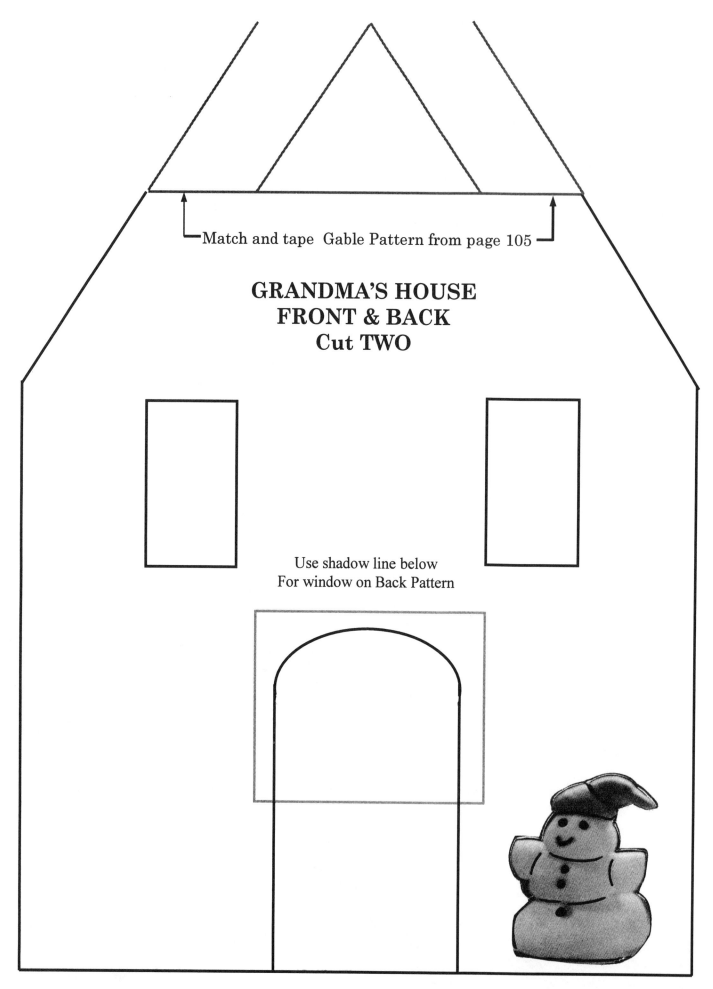

GRANDMA'S HOUSE – GABLE FRONT & BACK

Match and tape

Match and tape

Tape this Gable Pattern to Front and Back Pattern on the previous page.

GRANDMA'S HOUSE SIDE
Cut TWO

The Gingerbread tree pictured in front of Grandma's House is made with the Gingerbread Tree Centerpiece Pattern on Page 113.

BOTTOM

VICTORIAN HOUSE
Front Porch Roof - Cut ONE

(5-5/8" x 1-1/4")

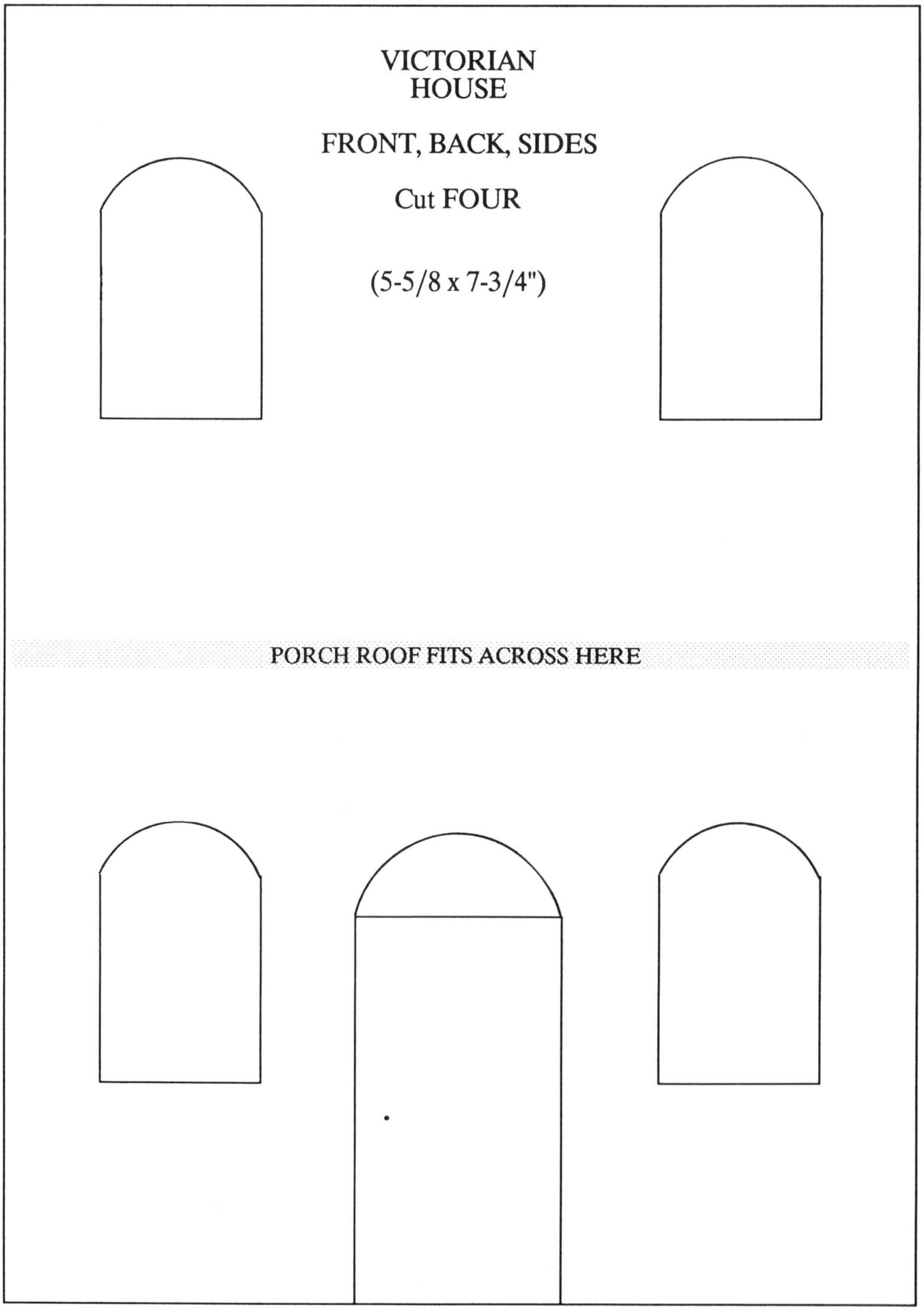

VICTORIAN HOUSE

FRONT, BACK, SIDES

Cut FOUR

(5-5/8 x 7-3/4")

PORCH ROOF FITS ACROSS HERE

**VICTORIAN
HOUSE
MAIN HOUSE ROOF SIDES
Cut FOUR**

(5-5/8" x 3-3/8" x 3-1/8")

**VICTORIAN HOUSE
FIRST ROOF – BASE
Cut ONE**

See a color picture of the Victorian Gingerbread House on Color Plate A

(6-1/2" x 6-1/2")

VICTORIAN HOUSE

TOP ROOF

(Cut ONE)

(4-1/8" x 4-1/8")

Victorian Window

Victorian House Door

SIDE PORCH ROOF

OR

SIDE PATIO "FLOOR"

Reinforce Gingerbread Roofs with Thin Styrofoam
or Cardboard (Held with Icing)

(5-5/8" x 3")

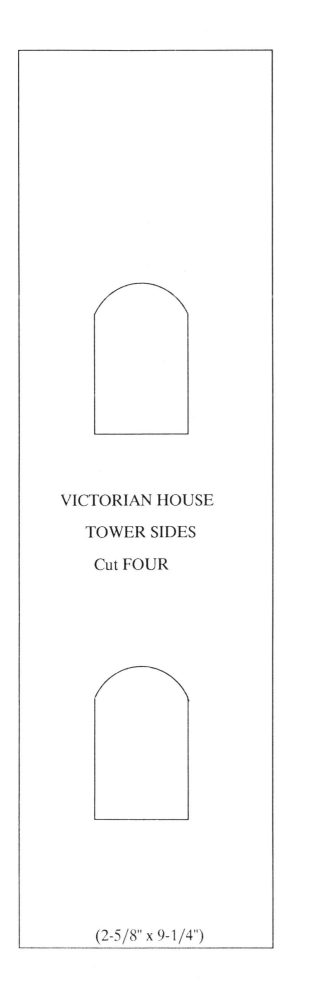
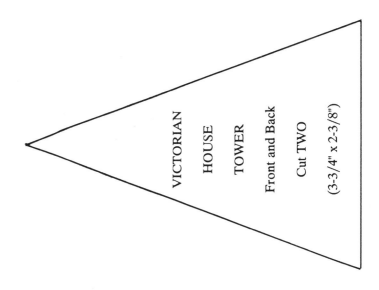

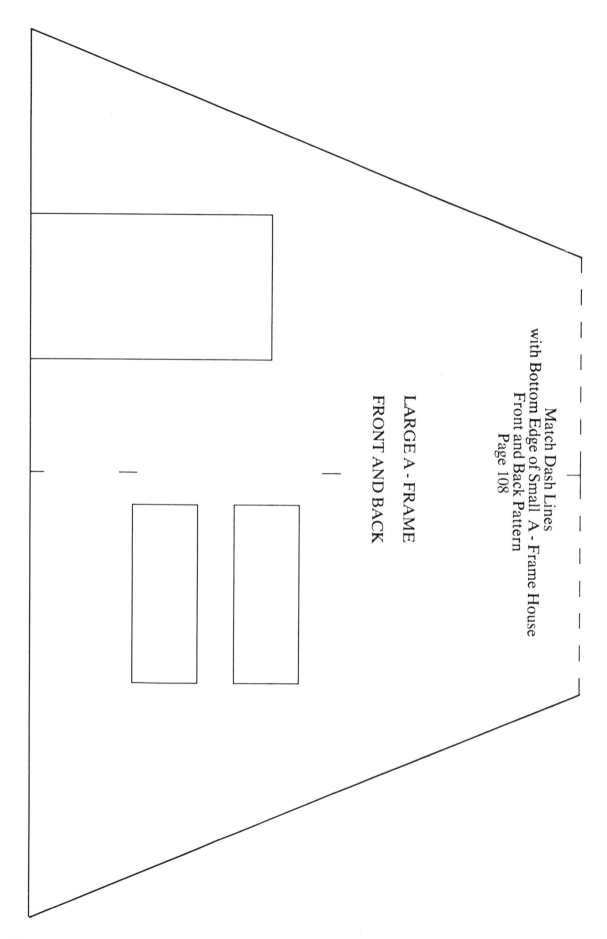

ONE - HALF
LARGE A - FRAME ROOF
Double Pattern on Dashed Lines
for
Total Size 8" x 12-3/4"

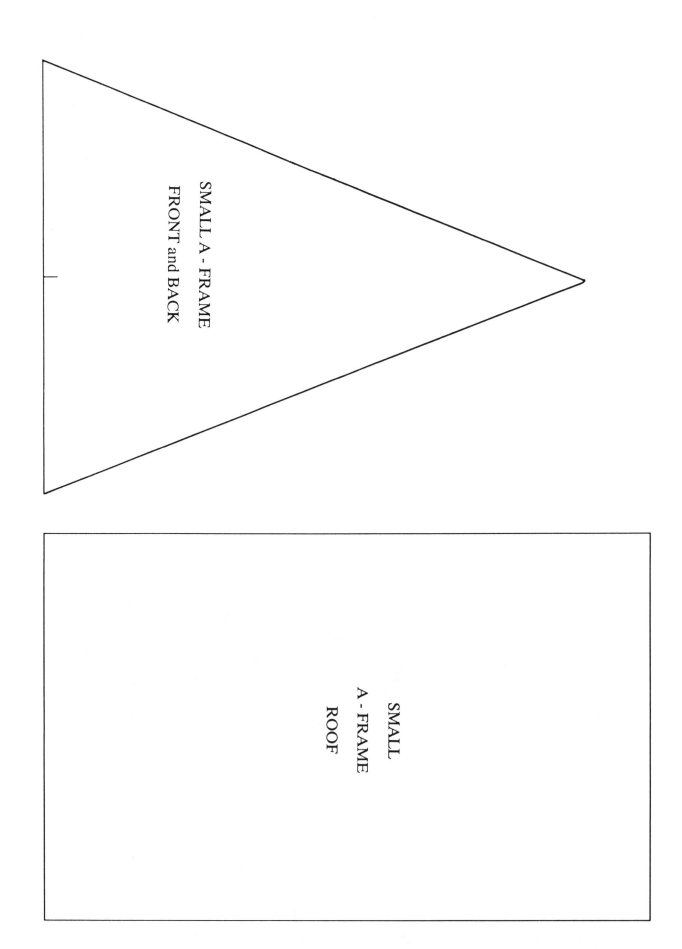

GINGERBREAD TREE CENTERPIECE PATTERN

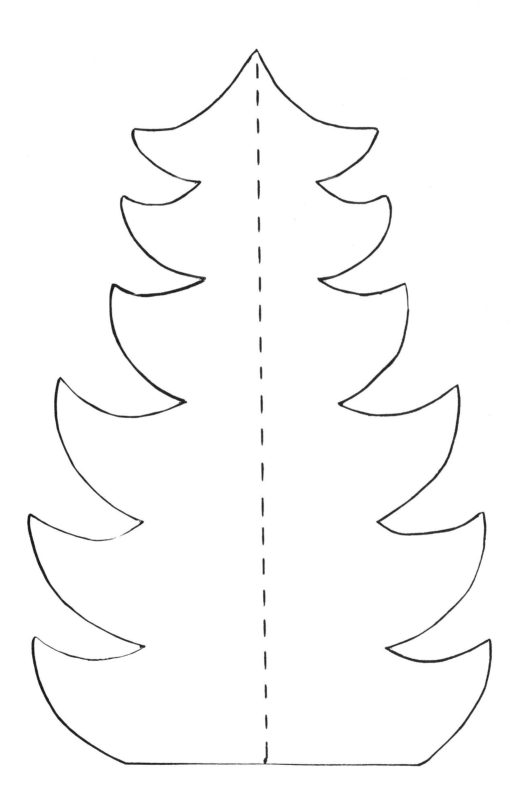

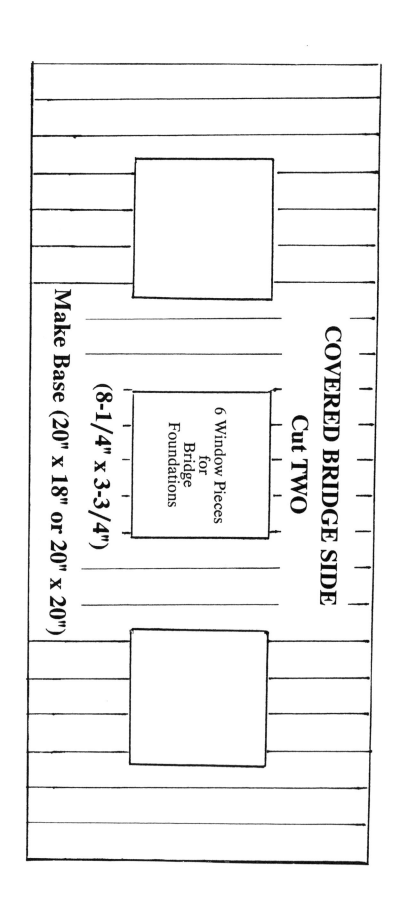

COVERED BRIDGE GINGERBREAD BASE
(8 1/2" x 4 3/4")
Cut ONE

See a color picture of the Gingerbread Covered Bridge on Color Plate B

115

COVERED BRIDGE ROOF
Cut TWO
(10 3/8" x 3-7/8")

BRIDGE WALL SUPPORTS
Cut FOUR
(1/2" x 3-1/2")

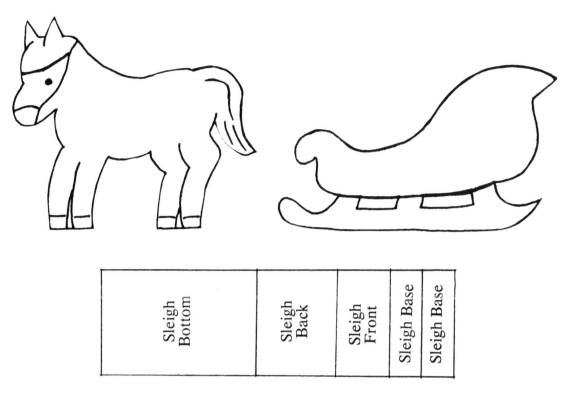

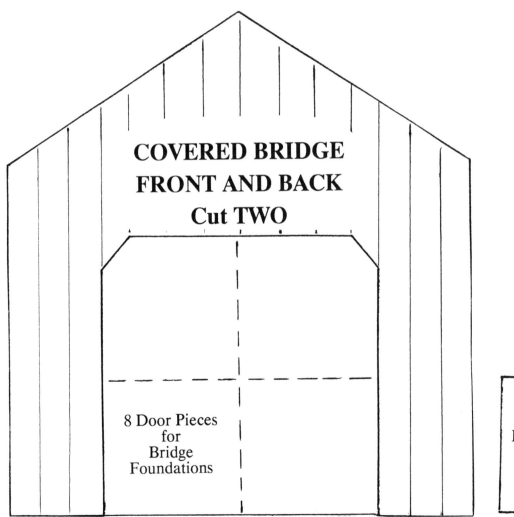

Make a Steeple of Cardboard to Support Gingerbread Steeple

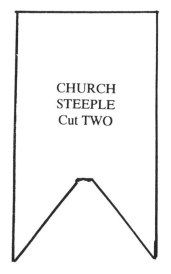

CHURCH STEEPLE Cut TWO

CHURCH STEEPLE SIDES Cut TWO

Small Round Window, Front and Back - Center Top

Two Large Windows Back of Church

CHURCH STEEPLE TOP Cut FOUR

Small Windows
Two on Each Side of Church
Two on Front on Each Side of Door

Trace Windows With White Icing on Waxed Paper Fill in With Yellow Icing (#3 Dec.Tip) Allow to Dry Overnight

GINGERBREAD CHURCH SIDES Cut TWO

Make Base (10" x 10" or larger)

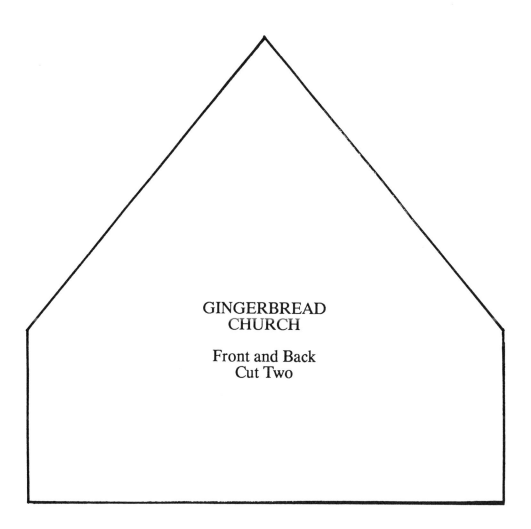

GINGERBREAD
CHURCH

Front and Back
Cut Two

GINGERBREAD CHURCH ROOF

Cut TWO

**SLEIGH BOTTOM
Cut ONE**

**SLEIGH BACK
Cut ONE**

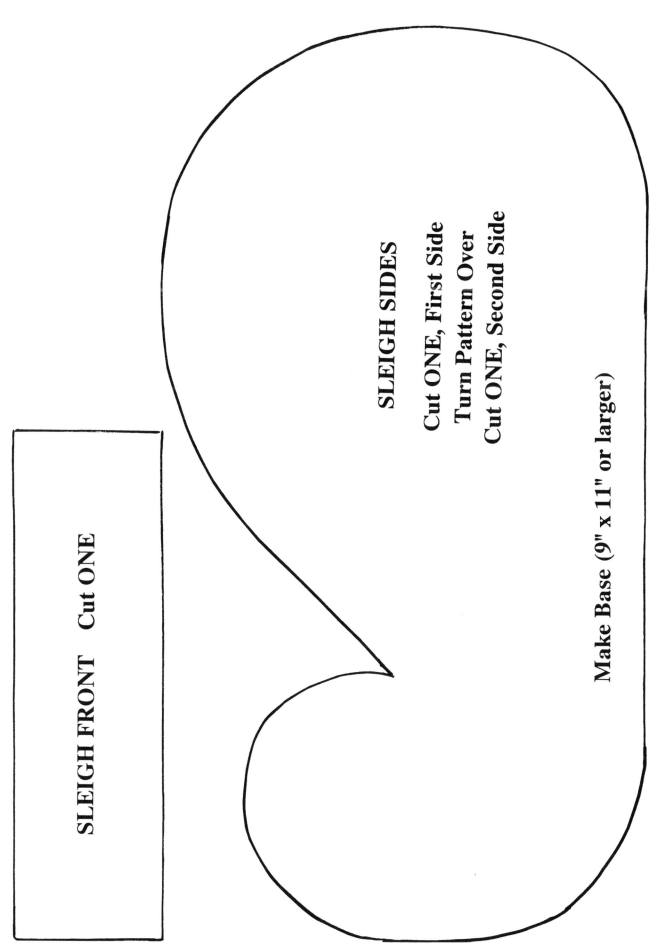

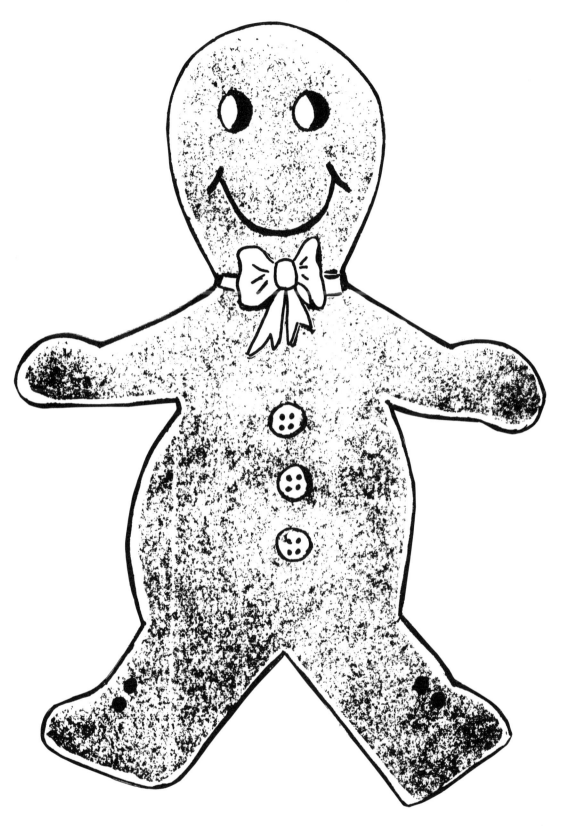

This pattern is perfect to make large gingerbread boy cookies (recipe on page 82). Trace the pattern on light weight cardboard or heavy brown paper. The pattern can also be used to cut out of brown construction paper for decorations. Hang paper boys on doors, windows, walls for a Gingerbread Party. These paper boys are charming when arranged "hand-to-hand".

MAIL ORDER RESOURCES

The following Mail Order Companies provide the listed resources:

<u>C</u>ake <u>A</u>nd <u>K</u>andy <u>E</u>mporium™
Village Common   2019 Miller Road   East Petersburg, PA 17520-1624
1-800-577-5728   717-569-5728
Parchment Paper Triangles, Metal Decorating Tubes, Plastic Couplers,
Meringue Powder, Liquid and Paste Food Colors, Marzapan,
Confectionery Coatings, Cookie Cutters
(Specializes in Candymaking including Clear Toy Candy)

Cambridge Career Products
1-800-468-4227
(1), (2), (3), (4)

Educational Media Company
Ontario, CANADA 905-873-7009
(2), (3), (4)

Instructional Video
1-800-228-0164
(2), (3), (4)

Library Video Company
1-800-843-3620
(2), (3), (4)

Professional Media Service Corp.
310-532-9024
(2), (3), (4)

The Gingerbread Lady, **Patti Hudson**
2714 Royal Road   Lancaster, PA 17603
717-394-8220
(1), (2), (3), (4)

1. ***Gingerbread Ideas*** book
2. **Gingerbread Land** video for children
3. ***The Joy of Gingerbread Housemaking*** video
4. ***The Gingerbread House,*** video

Notes

Notes